ENDURING FAITH®
Confirmation Curriculum

LEADER GUIDE

30-LESSON APOLOGETICS STUDY

CONCORDIA PUBLISHING HOUSE • SAINT LOUIS

Special thanks go to the pastors,
educators, and teachers of faith who
served as consultants for this curriculum.

3558 S. Jefferson Ave., St. Louis, MO 63118-3968
1-800-325-3040 • cph.org

Edited by Lisa M. Clark and Mark Sengele

Series editors: Pete Jurchen and Lisa A. Krenz

Manufactured in India/417564.

3 4 5 6 7 8 9 10 11 12   33 32 31 30 29 28 27 26 25 24

Contents

Unit 1: What Is Apologetics?

Timeless Truth

God has called me into the important role of defending the faith.

Essential Question

What is my role in sharing and defending the faith with those around me?

Focus Statements

1. The learner will explain how defending the faith is an important part of sharing life together with others.
2. The learner will describe different worldviews, particular philosophies of life or concepts of the world, and especially how a Christian worldview focuses on Christ and His work for us.
3. The learner will describe how the balance between, and proper use of, Law and Gospel are essential to the teaching of God's Word.
4. The learner will practice speaking the truth in a loving way.
5. The learner will be able to list the tools that are available for use when defending the faith.

Assessment Options

1. Preassessment Options

Before you begin this unit, have each learner spend a few minutes writing down or telling you or a partner personal responses to the following:

- Define what apologetics is.
- Explain what it means to defend the faith.
- List two important things to keep in mind when talking about Jesus with others.

After learners have finished, either collect the answers (to read and leave feedback) or quickly go over them together as a class. You'll get a sense of where each learner is coming from as you begin.

2. Formative Assessment Options

Formative assessments are ways to monitor learning. Checking for understanding and giving feedback improves both learning and instruction. Choose from the following:

a. Learning Log: After each class, have learners write in their Learning Log one important thing they discovered in that class. Space is available in the back of their Student Book for this. However, a small notebook may be a helpful option, especially if they take their Student Books home each week, so that you can review their comments regularly.

b. Reflection Tools: Since this is the first unit, now would be a good time to introduce the different self-reflection tools you plan to use throughout this course. By introducing these throughout this unit one by one and then having the learners keep them in their learning portfolios, you'll be able to check what learners do and do not yet understand.

3. Summative Assessment Options

Summative assessments evaluate learning at the end of an instructional unit. Choose from the following:

a. Learning Portfolio: A collection or portfolio of work may be a great option for checking for understanding at the end of each unit. For example, learners may complete checks for understanding at the end of each class. Learners who complete these tasks over the course of the unit will find them to be a great summative assessment. *Note:* At the beginning, provide a list of the samples you will collect so there are no surprises at the end.

b. Written Responses: Check for understanding by asking your learners to write short answers to several questions. This could be done inside or outside of class, and length of the answers can vary. However, this is not a good option for learners who struggle academically. Remember, your goal is to identify what has been learned, not writing skills, so allow modifications as needed. For example, some learners could dictate answers to questions to an adult or into a recording device.

   You may write your own questions, or use the following questions based on the unit:

   - What does it mean to defend the faith?
   - What is important to consider when sharing the faith with others?
   - Why is it important to consider worldview when defending the faith?

Teaching Tips

1 This unit is unique in this curriculum in that it spends more time preparing learners for apologetics than working through specific topics. In many ways, it sets the stage for discussion and activities later. For example, here learners will wrestle with understanding their worldview and speaking truth in love; those topics will come up throughout each lesson as they apply their learning and practice defending the faith to others.

2. Keep in mind that your learners will vary in their learning from topic to topic. Most likely, you are teaching this course to people who have already gone through a catechism study. If not, you'll need to work through more foundational knowledge from time to time. Other times, a lesson might revisit something learners know well but may still challenge them, as the lessons in this course come from an angle of articulating the faith to others. That said, there will be times when the learners themselves will need some convincing. In other words, it's critical that you use your discretion to pick and choose the parts of each lesson you want to spend time on, based on your learners' prior knowledge. Remember, you are aiming for learning. Always ask yourself: Do my learners better understand the content of the Timeless Truth and the Lesson Focus? How do I know? Keep returning to this.

3. This entire curriculum uses the 2017 edition of *Luther's Small Catechism with Explanation*. The references to the questions will match only with that edition. It's a good idea to keep a catechism or two available for your learners to use.

Color Key for Teacher Notes

Tan = Specific additional assessments

Blue = Extra activities or questions

Green = Educational tips and directions for specific activities

Gold = Explanations of theological concepts or background for the teacher

What Is Apologetics?

Timeless Truth

God has called me into the important role of defending the faith.

Lesson Focus

The learner will explain how defending the faith is an important part of sharing life together with others.

1 What Is Apologetics?

Consider This

Have you heard the word *apologetics* before? What do you think of when you hear this term?

The word *apologetics* sounds like the word *apology*. When we use the word *apology* today, it normally has to do with admitting error or regret. But it can also mean "to make a defense." When Christians study *apologetics*, they are actually referring to defending the faith, not apologizing for it.

Make a Defense

Read **1 Peter 3:15**. We will explore this passage and its context often throughout this course, but for now, write down important words that you notice in it.

Not of the World

Not everyone will agree with our Christian faith. What things have you noticed that are sometimes hard to talk about with your non-Christian friends?

Think About It . . .

Why is it important to defend our faith with gentleness and respect?

I can explain how defending the faith is an important part of sharing life together with others.

5

Unit 1: What Is Apologetics?

God has called me into the important role of defending the faith.

For this course, learners will probably fall on a very wide spectrum of learning readiness. Some will already be aware of the term as well as the need for apologetics. Some may actually need to hear why defending the faith is important. You may need to remind your learners of this importance at intervals throughout the course. At any point, if you feel that there is any confusion, make it "real." Ask: "Have you ever felt different because you are a Christian?" "Has anyone ever said to you . . . ?"

Feel free to do this activity together as a class. Read the verse out loud and write answers for all to see. Or pull the verse up on a projector and highlight terms that the learners point out.

This is a great "thermometer" opportunity to check the temperature of the room. Do learners assume that they should be accepted in society? Do learners feel like outsiders?

Remind learners that apologetics serves as a tool of evangelism, but never as the first approach. One should only apply apologetics when issues are raised. Always lead with the Law and the Gospel.

For longer Scripture passages (or even for shorter ones), remind learners that they can use a Bible app to listen rather than read.

For learners who struggle to synthesize big ideas or narratives, first talk with them about what they have read or heard in these verses; then help them organize their thoughts into concise words or pictures.

Digging Deeper

In This World . . .

Sometimes, Christians are surprised when things don't go their way. What does Jesus say about living as a Christian in this world? Read or listen to the following passages, and sum them up in your own words or sketches.

John 15:18–21, 26–27

John 16:33

1 Corinthians 1:23–25

You Will Have Trouble

We live in a fallen world filled with sin and trouble. Jesus tells us that our lives will not be easy, especially as Christians. Think of examples of trouble that Christians have faced throughout history and today.

If you have news articles or video clips handy, show learners real examples of hardships faced by Christians. Voice of the Martyrs (persecution.com) provides resources concerning challenges to the Gospel around the world.

As time permits, ask learners to line up against the wall as a visible spectrum to answer this question: "How much of a problem is persecution today?" Guide learners toward a careful balance to neither dismiss injustices toward Christians nor insist that religious freedom means a Christian theocracy.

EYES ON THE PRIZE

In a debate or sports game or battle, it is essential to prepare. It's good to keep in mind the objective, and it's also important to know your enemy. This apologetics class will help you prepare for defending your faith. So let's get our game plan together.

Whom are we fighting against? (See Romans 7:17; 1 Corinthians 15:26; 1 Peter 5:8–9.)

Opponent:

Why are we fighting in the first place? (See John 16:32–33.)

Objective:

GOD'S GAME PLAN

When we defend the faith, we need to remember the end goal that God has in mind. It is not for our sake or our glory. It is not to defend our honor. And the person or people we are talking with are not our opponent. In fact, they are the prize, people Jesus has died to save.

Using words, pictures, or sketches, read the Bible passage and describe the game plan for Christians until Jesus comes back.

Matthew 28:18–20

7

Help learners remember that our true enemies are sin, death, and the devil. This will change how we talk with others. They are not the enemy; they are the prize for whom Jesus died.

This also affects the objective. We do not defend the faith to prove others wrong. We do so in hopes that they hear and take to heart the saving Gospel.

God doesn't need us to defend Him or His Word. He wants us to be prepared to explain why we believe what we do. As learners go through this course, they will discover how to demonstrate the truth of God's Word as they share it with others.

There are plenty of ways the learners could do this activity: a checklist, word art, pictures.

If they get stuck, demonstrate the first portion. For example, write "Go" on the page; then draw a circle and an arrow from "Go" to the circle. Write "make disciples" on the arrow and "of all nations" in the circle. If learners focus on the action words, the rest will follow.

These workbooks are to guide and stimulate thinking, not for grading written responses. Some learners process better by thinking and writing; others process information better by talking through it. Let learners know that you are not "grading" their writing or looking at grammar and spelling. Help them to understand that the writing activities are here to help them process, think, and remember later.

If learners have trouble coming up with two things they learned, encourage them to review their answers to the other questions, especially for "Not Ashamed."

If you have adhesive notes or tabs, you may want to give each learner a tab to mark this page. If learners lose focus during other lessons on the importance of defending the faith, point them back to this page.

Connections

Not Ashamed

Sharing the Gospel can be a risky or scary thing to do. So why do Christians do it?

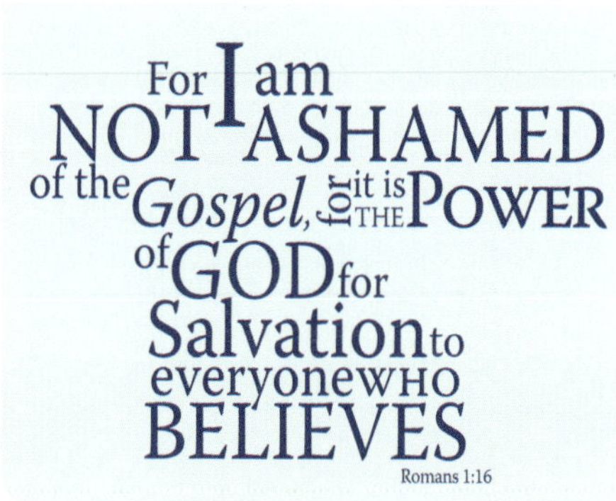

Sum It Up

List two important things you learned today about apologetics. What is one question you still have?

1.

2.

?

8

Checks for Understanding

Before your learners leave, consider ways you can give them feedback for next week.

- **Paired Discussion:** Ask learners to share with another learner at least one of the thoughts they wrote down in the "Sum It Up" section today.
- **Learning Log**: Ask learners to write one thing they hope to discover in this course. Use this preassessment as a guide as you go through the course together.

What Is a Worldview?

Timeless Truth

God has called me into the important role of defending the faith.

Lesson Focus

The learner will describe different worldviews, particular philosophies of life or concepts of the world, and especially how a Christian worldview focuses on Christ and His work for us.

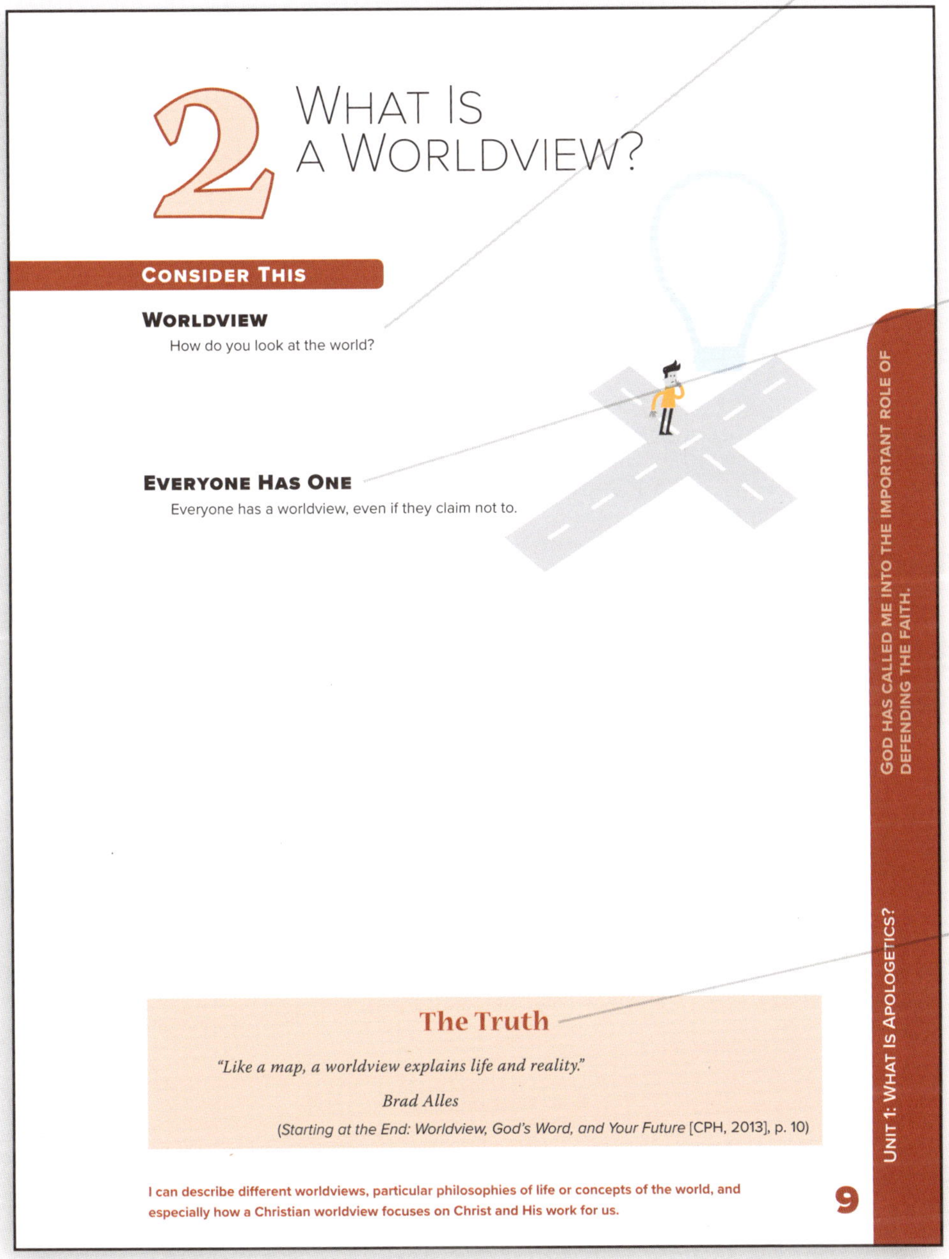

2 What Is a Worldview?

Consider This

Worldview

How do you look at the world?

Everyone Has One

Everyone has a worldview, even if they claim not to.

The Truth

"Like a map, a worldview explains life and reality."

Brad Alles

(*Starting at the End: Worldview, God's Word, and Your Future* [CPH, 2013], p. 10)

I can describe different worldviews, particular philosophies of life or concepts of the world, and especially how a Christian worldview focuses on Christ and His work for us.

9

Unit 1: What Is Apologetics?

God has called me into the important role of defending the faith.

Introduce the topic of worldview by having learners answer this question.

While our worldview may not be formalized, everyone has a worldview—a way in which they process and observe everything around them. Some learners may claim they don't have a worldview, but in reality, everyone has one.

Spend a few moments reviewing the quote from author and speaker Brad Alles. Discuss how a worldview can function as a map for us as we explore life.

Review the four parts of a worldview with learners. Help them understand each of the stages involved. Provide examples as needed to help learners with the next step of the process.

Digging Deeper

Parts of a Worldview

1. **Fundamental Assertion**
   Beliefs about whether God is or God isn't
2. **Philosophy**
   Beliefs about what reality is
3. **Ethics**
   Beliefs about how to behave
4. **Future**
   Beliefs about what goals life is moving toward (linear view of history)

This section of the lesson should take the longest to develop. Be sure to allow plenty of time for learners to outline the four sections of their personal worldview.

As time allows, discuss each worldview statement together with the whole group.

What's Your Worldview?

Fundamental Assertion

Philosophy

Ethics

Future

Some learners may need to talk this out to be able to process their thoughts and figure out what they believe. It might be helpful for many of your learners to do this as a group. If you've already done this as a group, sit down next to the learner who may need more guidance and coach him or her through these sections.

10

Testing Your Worldview

Does it fit the facts?

Does it have contradictions?

Is it useful in life?

11

The most important part of a worldview is to make sure it really works in practical applications. To help learners explore this concept further, take one or two worldviews and apply the tests to them.

For an example of a contradictory worldview, share secular humanism's stance on ethics, known as "moral relativism." Moral relativism states that there are no absolutes. In other words, it contradicts itself by stating absolutely that there is no such thing as an absolute.

Another example is the "naturalistic" worldview, where people believe only what they can perceive in nature, so thoughts and feelings are just the result of how the cells in our brains are firing. People with a naturalistic worldview believe in evolution.

Agnosticism: uncertainty about the existence of God

Atheism: denies the existence of God

Deism: God created the world and then left it alone

Humanism: no need for religious beliefs to behave in correct, moral, and ethical ways

Moralistic therapeutic deism: God exists to make people feel good and satisfy their needs

Pantheism: everything is God

If some of your learners have special needs that affect reading and comprehension, do the matching section together as a group or in small groups, where one person can find and read glossary terms as needed. These definitions may need to be explained more simply for some learners.

Connections

What's the Worldview?

Use the glossary in your catechism to match the worldview with the description.

Agnosticism	No need for religious beliefs to behave in correct, moral, and ethical ways
Atheism	Uncertain about the existence of God
Deism	God exists to make people feel good and satisfy their needs
Humanism	Denies the existence of God
Moralistic Therapeutic Deism	Everything is God
Pantheism	God created the world and then left it alone

Wrap It Up

Write a prayer for those whose worldview prevents them from seeing Jesus as their Savior. Share your prayer with the whole group.

12

Checks for Understanding

Before your learners leave, consider ways you can give them feedback for next week.

- **Learning Log:** In their Learning Log, have learners record two or three key points of their worldview.
- **Quiz Questions:** Have learners write a review question for this lesson. Use their questions to review at the start of the next lesson.

What Are Law and Gospel? Why Do They Matter?

Timeless Truth

God has called me into the important role of defending the faith.

Lesson Focus

The learner will describe how the balance between, and proper use of, Law and Gospel are essential to the teaching of God's Word.

3 What Are Law and Gospel? Why Do They Matter?

Consider This

Read **Questions 10** and **11** from the catechism and write your own answers to the two questions.

10. What are the two great doctrines of the Bible?

11. What is the difference between the Law and the Gospel?

I can describe how the balance between, and proper use of, Law and Gospel are essential to the teaching of God's Word.

13

UNIT 1: WHAT IS APOLOGETICS?

GOD HAS CALLED ME INTO THE IMPORTANT ROLE OF DEFENDING THE FAITH.

Remind learners that apologetics serves as a tool of evangelism, but never as the first approach. One should only apply apologetics when issues are raised. Always lead with the Law and the Gospel.

10. What are the two great doctrines of the Bible?

Law and Gospel are the two great doctrines of the Bible. We must sharply distinguish between the Law and the Gospel in order to understand the Bible rightly.

11. What is the difference between the Law and the Gospel?

The Law teaches what we are to do and not to do; the Gospel teaches what God has done, and still does, in Jesus, for our salvation.

The Law shows us our sin and the wrath of God; the Gospel shows us our Savior and brings God's grace and favor.

The Law must be proclaimed to all people, but especially to sinners who refuse to repent; the Gospel must be proclaimed to sinners who are troubled by their sins.

Keep an extra catechism handy for learners who are new to your group and who may not have gone through confirmation with your church.

Romans 3:20 *For by works of the Law no human being will be justified in His sight, since through the Law comes knowledge of sin.*

John 6:63 *It is the Spirit who gives life; the flesh is no help at all. The words that I have spoken to you are spirit and life.*

Romans 1:16 *For I am not ashamed of the gospel, for it is the power of God for salvation to everyone who believes, to the Jew first and also to the Greek.*

Digging Deeper

Where in the Word?

Why is understanding and being able to distinguish between Law and Gospel so important?

Romans 3:20

John 6:63

Romans 1:16

Apologetics serves as a tool of evangelism, but never as the first approach. One should only apply apologetics when issues are raised. Always lead with the Law and the Gospel.

What If?

What happens when we confuse the use of Law and Gospel?

14

Spend time discussing the importance of keeping Law and Gospel in their proper balance. Overemphasizing one over the other can lead away from the great gift God gives us in His Word.

Group discussion is the best way to share the content of this lesson. But what about learners who don't speak up quickly or who struggle with verbal expression? Think about ways to engage those learners.

Look online for some examples of "sketch notes" that you can show your learners. This visual form of note-taking might be a good nonverbal way for learners to participate.

Whose Job Is It?

Who is responsible for making sure that Law and Gospel are used properly?

2 Timothy 2:15

2 Corinthians 4:2

Colossians 1:4–6

In Him we have obtained an inheritance, having been predestined according to the purpose of Him who works all things according to the counsel of His will, so that we who were the first to hope in Christ might be to the praise of His glory. In Him you also, when you heard the word of truth, the gospel of your salvation, and believed in Him, were sealed with the promised Holy Spirit, who is the guarantee of our inheritance until we acquire possession of it, to the praise of His glory.

Ephesians 1:11–14

15

2 Timothy 2:15 *Do your best to present yourself to God as one approved, a worker who has no need to be ashamed, rightly handling the word of truth.*

2 Corinthians 4:2 *But we have renounced disgraceful, underhanded ways. We refuse to practice cunning or to tamper with God's word, but by the open statement of the truth we would commend ourselves to everyone's conscience in the sight of God.*

Colossians 1:4–6 *We heard of your faith in Christ Jesus and of the love that you have for all the saints, because of the hope laid up for you in heaven. Of this you have heard before in the word of the truth, the gospel, which has come to you, as indeed in the whole world it is bearing fruit and increasing—as it also does among you, since the day you heard it and understood the grace of God in truth.*

If your learners have their Bibles with them, encourage them to highlight these passages in their Bibles for future use.

Psalm 94:12 *Blessed is the man whom You discipline, O LORD, and whom You teach out of Your law.* LAW

Matthew 5:17 *Do not think that I have come to abolish the Law or the Prophets; I have not come to abolish them but to fulfill them.* GOSPEL

Luke 10:25–27 *And behold, a lawyer stood up to put Him to the test, saying, "Teacher, what shall I do to inherit eternal life?" He said to him, "What is written in the Law? How do you read it?" And He answered, "You shall love the Lord your God with all your heart and with all your soul and with all your strength and with all your mind, and your neighbor as yourself."* LAW

John 1:17 *For the law was given through Moses; grace and truth came through Jesus Christ.* GOSPEL

Romans 3:27–31 *Then what becomes of our boasting? It is excluded. By what kind of law? By a law of works? No, but by the law of faith. For we hold that one is justified by faith apart from works of the law. Or is God the God of Jews only? Is he not the God of Gentiles also? Yes, of Gentiles also, since God is one—who will justify the circumcised by faith and the uncircumcised through faith. Do we then overthrow the law by this faith? By no means! On the contrary, we uphold the law.* GOSPEL

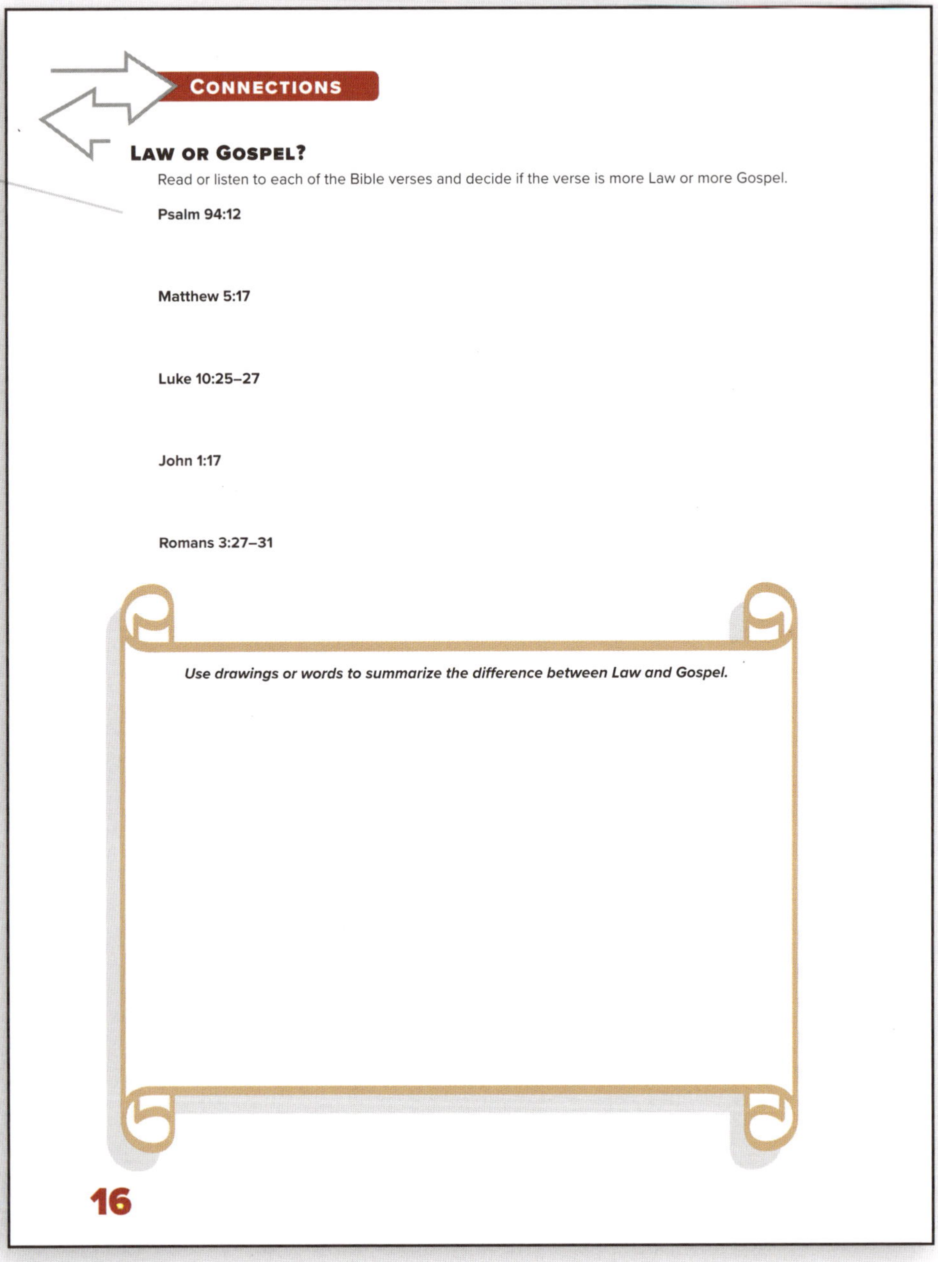

CONNECTIONS

LAW OR GOSPEL?

Read or listen to each of the Bible verses and decide if the verse is more Law or more Gospel.

Psalm 94:12

Matthew 5:17

Luke 10:25–27

John 1:17

Romans 3:27–31

Use drawings or words to summarize the difference between Law and Gospel.

16

CHECKS FOR UNDERSTANDING

Before your learners leave, consider ways you can give them feedback for next week.

- **Learning Log:** In their Learning Log, have learners record their favorite Bible verses and decide if that verse is more Law or more Gospel.
- **Exit Ticket:** Have learners review the lyrics of a favorite hymn and identify the Law and Gospel in the lyrics.

How Do We Speak the Truth in Love with Our Neighbor?

Timeless Truth

God has called me into the important role of defending the faith.

Lesson Focus

The learner will practice speaking the truth in a loving way.

4 How Do We Speak the Truth in Love with Our Neighbor?

Consider This

Truth in Love

Read or listen to the following Bible verses.

Ephesians 4:15

1 John 3:18

2 John 1:3–5

Discuss why you think these Bible passages include both truth and love.

One or the Other?

It can be tempting to use "truth" as an excuse to not be loving. It can also be tempting to use "love" as an excuse to not be truthful. How might you respond to the following?

"I don't care what other people think. I'm right, and I'm just telling it like it is. If they don't like it, they must not like me. Or truth. Or even God."

"Who cares what's right or wrong? It doesn't really matter as long as we all get along. I like kind people. And I want people to know that I'm not judging them. That's all that really matters."

I can speak the truth in a loving way.

17

Unit 1: What Is Apologetics?

God has called me into the important role of defending the faith.

Consider a "What Would You Do?" opener. Ask the following questions, or make some of your own. You may want to divide the class into smaller groups to foster a game feel. The objective is for learners to understand the importance of both truth and love. Either use the multiple choices at first, or wait and use them to extend the discussion.

Your toddler cousin is running toward a campfire. What would you do?

a. Let her go. She'll get mad if you stop her.

b. Yell at her for being so dumb.

c. Run and stop her, telling her that fire is hot.

Your friend is about to jump off a fifteen-foot wall on his bike. What would you do?

a. See what happens. It's his choice.

b. Tell him that he's too stupid to be your friend and leave.

c. Remind him that you don't want him to get hurt; ask for help from a nearby adult.

This last question might offer a great opportunity to ask learners if they've seen examples of Christians sharing the truth in ways that are not loving. Social media is often a natural place for short, even condescending, remarks to distract from the truth of a message.

Remember this "truth in love" phrase and use it throughout the course as learners practice responses to various issues.

Digging Deeper

Truth or Love?

What does God say about truth? What does He say about love? Read the following, and jot down some thoughts.

John 8:31–32

1 John 4:7–8

The truth is, we are not loving our neighbors if we keep them from the truth of Jesus. Even though it can be tough, telling the truth can be the most loving thing you can do. Give some examples of hard truths that people need to hear.

Truth without love isn't very truthful. How can we represent God, who is love, if we are not telling the truth in a loving way? Sure, that love can sometimes be tough love (think of a parent who disciplines a toddler for running toward a stove). But using honesty as an excuse to be mean isn't honest at all. Give some examples of why a loving approach is important when talking with others, especially when talking about the truth of God.

18

Explain Everything in the Kindest Way

The discussion of speaking the truth in love comes up when considering the Eighth Commandment. In the Small Catechism, read through **Question 86** and its answer.

Let's think about what we've learned so far about Law and Gospel, worldview, and the whole point behind apologetics in the first place. Consider the following sentence:

"It matters what you say AND how you say it."

Do you agree? disagree? Why?

Gentleness and Respect

If you remember much about the disciple Peter, you'll probably remember that he could be impulsive, often saying things without really thinking. Later on in his life, however, he gave this advice in a letter:

> *Now who is there to harm you if you are zealous for what is good? But even if you should suffer for righteousness' sake, you will be blessed. Have no fear of them, nor be troubled, but in your hearts honor Christ the Lord as holy, always being prepared to make a defense to anyone who asks you for a reason for the hope that is in you; yet do it with gentleness and respect, having a good conscience, so that, when you are slandered, those who revile your good behavior in Christ may be put to shame. For it is better to suffer for doing good, if that should be God's will, than for doing evil.* 1 Peter 3:13–17

Highlight or circle words that jump out at you or that seem important. What is Peter trying to say?

19

This section attempts to bring together all the things learned so far. If needed, back up a little and walk through Question 86, or save this question until later. After learners practice the activity on the next page, they may be better prepared to articulate a response here.

The idea of respecting the opinion and beliefs of others is a hallmark of the current generation. While this concept sounds good, it rarely seems to play out in real-life application. It seems that instead of having civil conversations to explain our differences, more people try to yell past one another to see who can yell the loudest.

The problem is, with all the yelling, no one can hear what either side is saying. As Christians, we want others to hear the Good News of Jesus Christ, so we speak with gentleness and respect. The loud cacophony of the world makes this message hard to hear, so we are always alert for moments of silence when others can finally hear our gentle message.

Be sensitive to learners who may have family members who aren't Christian or who identify as Christian but are living outside of God's will (e.g., in a sexual relationship outside of marriage, often speaks ill of others and of God, sees nothing wrong with stealing or swindling others, doesn't attend church services, etc.). That doesn't mean you don't talk about these topics, but it certainly brings to the fore the importance of gentleness and respect.

CONNECTIONS

PRACTICE TIME

Take a look at the following statements. How might you say them in your own words, using truth in love?

If you don't read the Bible, you don't care about God.

Jesus loves everyone, no matter what.

Anyone who isn't a Christian is stupid.

SUM IT UP

List two important things you learned today about apologetics. What is one question you still have?

1.

2.

?

20

CHECKS FOR UNDERSTANDING

Before your learners leave, consider ways you can give them feedback for next week.

- **Note for Home:** Ask learners to write a note to their family, explaining the lesson today. Tell learners to share the note with their family during the week. If you think the notes won't make it into the homes, collect them and send them yourself.
- **Video Review:** Have families create their own review video for the lesson. Encourage each family member to share something he or she learned in this lesson.

What Tools Do We Use When We Defend the Faith?

Timeless Truth

God has called me into the important role of defending the faith.

Lesson Focus

The learner will be able to list the tools that are available for use when defending the faith.

If you have many concrete learners, bring some concrete examples to class. Hold up a saw and tell them they are going to paint the wall. Or hold up a needle and thread and tell them that you are going to build a table. Emphasize that you need the right tool for the job, and that's the case with defending the faith too.

5 What Tools Do We Use When We Defend the Faith?

Consider This

The Tools for the Job

Let's say you're researching the best phone to buy. Where do you go for help? *Circle all that apply.*

Online reviews ▪ Videos of tech experts ▪ Your friends ▪ Your three-year-old sister ▪ Your teacher

Now, you're studying for your history test. Where do you go for help? *Circle all that apply.*

Your history book ▪ Your class notes ▪ Your friends ▪ Your teacher ▪ Social media

Now, you have questions about faith. Where do you turn for help? *Circle all that apply.*

Your pastor ▪ Your church ▪ The Bible ▪ Prayer ▪ Small Catechism ▪ Social media ▪ Your parents ▪ Your friends

Who's Got Your Back?

Your faith impacts your entire worldview. What you know about God impacts the way you see yourself, others, and even the end of the world. And when you defend the faith, you need backup. So why does it matter what tools you use for the job?

This question might take some time to process. Let learners write their own answer first. Then, ask pairs to share. Finally, open the question up to the whole group.

I can list the tools that are available for use when defending the faith.

21

Unit 1: What Is Apologetics? God has called me into the important role of defending the faith.

This spread gives more information than usual. To keep things exciting, remind learners that these tools are essential for their mission of defending the faith. Maybe use sports, soldiers, or another metaphor. Give your class a team name. Give each learner a personal title. This unit has been a basic training of sorts. Build momentum that they're about to dig in and prepare for some real battles.

For learners who aren't strong readers, read Bible passages aloud or teach learners to use a Bible app for listening or reading in bigger font.

Digging Deeper

Tool #1:

The Bible

If you want to know about God, who should you ask first? God, of course! God didn't create all of us and then just let us sit around, figuring out things on our own. No, God loves us and wants us to know who He is. So He gave us His Word, which is recorded in the Bible. Now, there are plenty of reasons why we trust the Bible as God's Word, and we'll get into that in later lessons. But as Christians, we trust that God is who He says He is. Here are a few examples of what God says about Himself and His Word.

Exodus 3:13–15

Isaiah 55:10–11

John 5:39

Tool #2:

Luther's Small Catechism with Explanation

Five hundred years ago, many Christians were not looking to the Bible for answers. And they didn't know the basics of the Christian faith. Martin Luther wrote the Small Catechism so that families could learn the faith. Luther used a question-and-answer style to help believers defend the faith. He always pointed to the Bible for the answers. After all, *sola Scriptura* (Scripture alone) was a huge focus for Luther's teaching. We go to the Bible for our answers, and we use tools like the Small Catechism to help us navigate what the Bible says. The Explanation included with the Small Catechism helps believers work through questions about faith that we have today.

Page through *Luther's Small Catechism with Explanation*. Look at some of the numbered Questions. What is always included in the answers?

22

Tool #3:

Other Believers

The Early Church had a lot of work to do. In order to spread the Word, they needed to talk to many different people and face all kinds of challenges and dangers. The New Testament is filled with passages in which believers are told to build up one another. Defending the faith isn't easy, and we can't do it alone. One of the blessings we have is the gift of fellow Christians. Who are some believers you talk with when you have questions?

1.

2.

3.

4.

5.

Tool #4:

Evidence

Sometimes, science, history, and even our own reason can help us understand and defend what we know to be true. Creation around us proclaims that there is a Creator, and the more we learn about our world, the more we realize how amazing God is. Gifts such as learning, recorded thoughts, and a good mind can be helpful tools for apologetics.

Use a search tool to find a Bible passage that talks about God being Lord of all creation.

Tools 2, 3, and 4 are helpful only as much as they serve Tool 1. Again, we turn to God's Word—*sola Scriptura*—as our ultimate authority. The Small Catechism is helpful because it points to the Bible. Fellow believers are trustworthy if and when they say things that fit with the Bible. Our own brains are incredible gifts from God, but when we get confused, we turn to God's Word.

Plus, we're not alone . . .

23

If there is a particular kind of team sport that is popular in your area or that your learners are especially interested in, try to use the analogy of comparing the believers that learners have listed here to the positions involved in the starting lineup of that sport (e.g., soccer, basketball, or football starting lineup). If your learners aren't interested in sports, talk about another type of group or activity where participants support one another, like a theater group or a band.

For learners who aren't strong writers, remind them that these pages will not be graded on spelling or grammar; the writing tasks are for getting thoughts down and processing information.

Connections

Our Helper

You are not alone. Yes, you have great tools. But you also have the Helper, the Holy Spirit. Jesus left His followers but promised that a Helper, the Holy Spirit, would come. When you pray, the Holy Spirit is helping you. When you read the Bible, the Holy Spirit is helping you. When you are telling others about Jesus, the Holy Spirit is helping you. Look at the Bible passages below. Think of three words about the Holy Spirit.

John 15:26 **John 3:5–6** **Psalm 104:30**

1.

2.

3.

Game Prep

Now, you know the importance of defending the faith (Lesson 1). You've learned tactics (Lessons 2 and 3) and approach strategies (Lesson 4). You know the opponent. You know the objective (Lesson 4). You have the tools, and you have the Helper (Lesson 5). It's time to dig in and equip yourself to defend the faith!

Before you go, what is your mission? What is your goal? Write or draw your answer below.

If you've been talking about teams, ask learners to record their quest or mission, their team name, and maybe a seal or emblem.

Sum It Up

What tools do you use when you want to know more about God? What question do you still wonder about today?

24

Checks for Understanding

Before your learners leave, consider ways you can give them feedback for next week.

- **Quest or Charter:** Make a big deal of learners leaving today, reinforcing that they are now ready for the tasks during the rest of the course. Ask learners to sign a class charter, recite their mission, or something similar as they leave.
- **Tools:** After learners write in the last box of the lesson, ask them to share their answers with one another. Maybe work together as a group to create a small poster listing all the tools. Post it in the classroom for the rest of the year.

Unit 2: Jesus

Timeless Truth

Jesus lives and has redeemed me to be His own.

Essential Question

What do I need to know about Jesus?

Focus Statements

6. The learner will share evidence beyond Scripture for the existence of Jesus as a real person.
7. The learner will express that Jesus is Lord and that what He says is true.
8. The learner will share evidence that the death and resurrection of Jesus were real events, witnessed by many people.
9. The learner will share with others ways that Jesus keeps His promises and how He will make all things new when He returns.

Assessment Options

1. **Preassessment Options**

   Before you begin this unit, have each learner spend a few minutes writing or telling you or a partner answers to the following questions:

   - Who is Jesus?
   - Can we believe what Jesus says to be true?
   - What will happen when Jesus comes again?

   After they have written these, either collect the answers (to read and leave feedback) or quickly go over them together as a class. You'll get a sense of where each learner is coming from as you begin.

2. **Formative Assessment Options**

   Formative assessments are ways to monitor learning. Choose from the following:

   a. Learning Log: After each class, have learners write in their Learning Log one important thing they discovered in that class. Space is available in the back of their Student Book for this. However, a small notebook may be a helpful option, especially if they take their Student Books home each week, so that you can review their comments regularly.

   b. Reflection Tools: Since this is the second unit, if you have not already introduced these tools, now would be a good time. Help learners utilize tools such as memory work and self-reflections. Now is also a good time to have them build their learning portfolios by adding these assessments as they go.

3. **Summative Assessment Options**

   Summative assessments evaluate learning at the end of an instructional unit. Choose from the following:

   a. Learning Portfolio: Have learners complete a variety of formative assessments over the course of this unit. At the end of the unit, they will compile at least one of each type of formative assessment, along with completed lesson notes and other samples you require. Learners who complete these tasks over the course of the unit will find them to be a great summative assessment. *Note*: At the beginning of the unit, provide a list of the samples you will collect so there are no surprises at the end.

   b. Written Responses: You can check for understanding by asking your learners to write short answers to several questions. This could be done inside or outside of class, and the length of answers can vary. However, this is not a good option for learners who struggle academically. Remember, your goal is to identify what has been learned, not writing skills, so allow modifications as needed. For example, some learners could dictate answers to questions to an adult or into a recording device.

You may write your own questions, or use the following questions based on the unit:

- How do we know that Jesus exists?
- Can we trust that Jesus died and rose from the dead?
- If Jesus is God, how should we treat His words?

Teaching Tips

1. This unit is foundational to the lessons that come after. It may seem strange that the creation is not one of the first lessons. But Jesus is easily proven as a real person. And there is also evidence to defend that Jesus truly rose from the dead. If Jesus is who He says He is, He can serve as the authority on many points, including the validity of the Bible itself. Because others may have a different worldview, Christians first need to establish that Jesus is to be trusted before we can use the Bible as proof of anything.
2. Remember that your learners will vary in their learning from topic to topic. Most likely, you are teaching this course to learners who have already gone through a catechism study. If not, you'll need to work through more foundational knowledge from time to time. Other times, a lesson might revisit something learners know well but may still challenge them, as the lessons in this course come from an angle of articulating the faith to others. That said, there will be times when the learners themselves will need some convincing. In other words, it's critical that you use your discretion to pick and choose the parts of each lesson you want to spend time on, based on your learners' prior knowledge. Remember, you are aiming for learning. Always ask yourself: Do my learners better understand the content of the Timeless Truth and the Lesson Focus? How do I know? Keep returning to this.
3. Again, this entire curriculum uses the 2017 edition of *Luther's Small Catechism with Explanation*. The references to the Questions will match only with that edition. It's a good idea to keep a catechism or two available for your learners to use.

Color Key for Teacher Notes

Tan = Specific additional assessments

Blue = Extra activities or questions

Green = Educational tips and directions for specific activities

Gold = Explanations of theological concepts or background for the teacher

Did Jesus Even Exist?

Timeless Truth

Jesus lives and has redeemed me to be His own.

Lesson Focus

The learner will share evidence beyond Scripture for the existence of Jesus as a real person.

6

Did Jesus Even Exist?

For there is one God, and there is one mediator between God and men, the man Christ Jesus.
1 Timothy 2:5

Consider This

In his letter to young Timothy, Paul calls the mediator between God and people "the man Christ Jesus." By faith, we know Jesus as our Lord and Savior. However, in this lesson, we will explore evidence for the existence of Jesus outside of the Scriptures.

Why might you want to prove the existence of Jesus?

True knowledge of Christ as Savior comes through God's Word by the power of the Holy Spirit. But when faith is challenged, it can be reassuring to be able to defend our faith by seeing evidence of Jesus' existence.

A Reliable Witness

Possible sources for historic evidence of the existence of Jesus:

Classical Greek or Roman writings and testimonies

Jewish Scriptures and other writings

Christian Scriptures, writings, and testimonies

What are the potential pros and cons of using these sources when attempting to prove the existence of Jesus?

Classical Greeks and Romans were likely hostile toward Jesus and had a definite bias against Christians.

Jewish people of the first century were also hostile toward Jesus and His ministry.

Christian biblical evidence for Jesus is considered biased by some because it comes from committed believers rather than neutral sources.

For your discussion of the pros and cons of using these sources, draw a T chart on the board with pros on one side and cons on the other. Write the pros and cons that your group suggests and add your own as you deem appropriate.

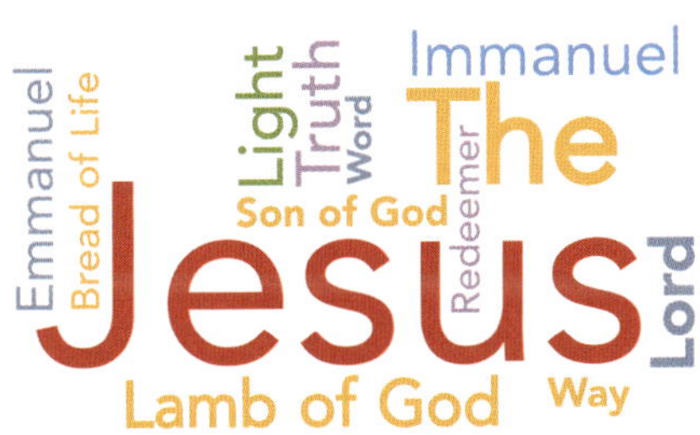

I can share that there is evidence beyond Scripture for the existence of Jesus as a real person.

Jesus lives and has redeemed me to be His own.

Unit 2: Jesus

25

Since early Christian witnesses could be considered biased, we will only explore Classical and Jewish accounts. Review the information together with learners.

Option: Look up these people online and find historical art to give learners a visual connection.

Possible answers:

1. He existed as a man.
2. His personal name was Jesus.
3. He was called Christus in Greek.
4. He had a brother named James.
5. He won over both Jews and Greeks.
6. Jewish leaders of that day expressed unfavorable opinions about Him.
7. Pilate rendered a decision the He should be executed.
8. His execution was specifically by crucifixion.
9. He was executed during Pontius Pilate's governorship over Judea.

Note: The vital evidence of Jesus' resurrection will be discussed in Lesson 8.

List responses where learners can see and copy.

Digging Deeper

Classical (Greek or Roman)

Caius Cornelius Tacitus was a Roman senator, orator, and historian. In his *Annals* (written about AD 116–17), Tacitus recorded how Nero shifted the blame for the burning of Rome to the "Chrestians," whose founder, Christus (Latin for *Christ*), was executed by Pontius Pilate during the reign of Tiberius.

Jewish

Josephus was a first-century Jewish priest who lived in Rome under the patronage of three successive Roman emperors. Josephus was a traitor by fellow Jews for his involvement with the Roman leaders. Josephus authored two great books, *The Jewish War* and *Jewish Antiquities*, both written in Greek for an educated audience. Some versions of *The Jewish War* mention Jesus, but scholars suspect these references were added by others.

In *Jewish Antiquities*, Josephus talks about the execution of James, the leader of the Church in Jerusalem. He specifically identifies James as the brother of Jesus, "who is called Christ." This reference makes sense only if Jesus was a real person.

A longer reference in *Jewish Antiquities* is known as the *Testimonium Flavianum*. This passage talks about the surprising deeds performed by Jesus and how He won over many Jews and Greeks with His teaching. Josephus remarks that Jesus' followers were still around to that day. Some experts question whether the passages referring to Jesus as the Messiah and the fulfillment of prophesy are all Josephus's writing. Even without these specific phrases, though, there is still sufficient evidence for Jesus' existence as a man.

Evidence Summary

Review the evidence presented by the Classical and Jewish witnesses and summarize below.

1.
2.
3.
4.
5.

26

Matching the Evidence

Use your Bible or online Bible tools to find verses to support each of the evidence statements from the Classical and Jewish witnesses.

His personal name was Jesus.

Jesus had a brother named James.

Jesus was called Christus in Greek.

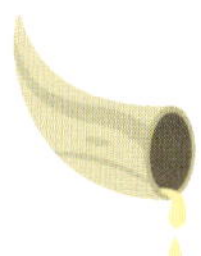

Jewish leaders of that day expressed unfavorable opinions about Jesus.

Pilate rendered a decision that Jesus should be executed.

Jesus' execution was specifically by crucifixion.

27

Possible answers:

His personal name was Jesus—Matthew 1:21, 25.

Jesus was called Christus in Greek—Matthew 16:16; Mark 8:29.

Jesus had a brother named James—Matthew 13:55; Mark 6:3.

Jewish leaders of that day expressed unfavorable opinions about Jesus—Matthew 9:11; Matthew 12:14.

Pilate rendered a decision that Jesus should be executed—Matthew 27:24.

Jesus' execution was specifically by crucifixion—Matthew 27:35; Matthew 28:5.

Learners who struggle with reading or who are not familiar with using Bible concordance or Bible app tools will need some guidance for this activity. If you know this will be the case, prepare the list of Bible verses provided here prior to class (perhaps on note cards) and have learners match them to the boxes on the page. Another option would be to read the text aloud for learners.

Allow time for learners to develop a plan for sharing the information they learned in this lesson. If time is tight, they could complete this activity on their own at home.

For learners who struggle to express their thoughts in writing, have them tell you their plan first and then you can write it for them. Or try having them use a digital device that they are accustomed to using to share their ideas.

CONNECTIONS

MAKE A PLAN

Consider your friends or family who doubt the reality of Jesus. Write a plan for how you could share with them some of the information you learned in this lesson. Remember that a gentle response works better than an attack on other people's unbelief.

28

CHECKS FOR UNDERSTANDING

Before your learners leave, consider ways you can give them feedback for next week.

- **Paired Discussion:** Ask learners to share at least one of the thoughts they have about the extrabiblical evidence for Christ.
- **Learning Log**: Ask learners to write something new that they learned in the lesson today.

Who Is Jesus?

Timeless Truth

Jesus lives and has redeemed me to be His own.

Lesson Focus

The learner will express that Jesus is Lord and that what He says is true.

If your learners have already taken a catechism study course, you have already discussed Jesus as Savior at length. This lesson, of course, is structured to equip learners who want to find ways to defend their faith when asked about Jesus. Even so, some learners may still have their own doubts or questions. Note where your learners stand. If your class is largely on the same page, you can breeze through the middle two pages and use the last page to dig into the Small Catechism Questions. If your learners are struggling, take more time with the middle two pages, and use the last page as a segue to the next lesson.

7 Who Is Jesus?

Consider This

In the previous lesson, we established that Jesus exists and lived in human form on this earth. There's just too much evidence from people who didn't have any reason to lie about Him for us to doubt that He is a real person. But what's the big deal? Who is Jesus?

Jesus asked His disciples the very same question.

"Who do others say that I am?"
So what do you think?

He also asked them a more important question.
"Who do you say that I am?"

Lunatic, Liar, or Lord

An author named C. S. Lewis started out as a determined atheist. He became a Christian (cool story, look it up sometime). At one point, he basically said that no one can really get away with calling Jesus a nice guy or a good teacher. Jesus is recorded as telling people that He is the Messiah. The disciples are recorded as dying for this same truth. So there's no way we can just have a halfway opinion about him. C. S. Lewis summarized that there are three possibilities about Jesus: He must be a lunatic, a liar, or the Lord. If He really did exist (Lesson 6), and if He claims to be God, He must be crazy, lying, or truly the Son of God. Let's explore those options.

Jesus lives and has redeemed me to be His own.

Unit 2: Jesus

I can express that Jesus is Lord and that what He says is true.

29

You can also look at the account in which the Pharisees, fully knowing that the guards reported a risen Christ, still lied and tried to cover it up (Matthew 28:11–15). It is not included here because the next lesson deals more with Jesus' death and resurrection. However, it could help pave the way for the next lesson.

For learners who aren't strong readers, Scripture reading can be perplexing, and they may find it embarrassing to read aloud. Read these passages aloud for them or allow learners to listen to passages on a Bible app. Even learners who are good readers can benefit from listening while they read along silently.

For learners who struggle with writing, use these questions for discussion without insisting that learners write answers in small spaces.

Digging Deeper

Liar

If Jesus were a liar, a false prophet, the Pharisees and Jewish leaders would have been totally justified in trying to get rid of Jesus for the sake of the people. After all, if Jesus was turning people away from God, there would be eternal consequences for God's people. But were the Pharisees right in saying that Jesus was a liar? Did they even really think He *was* a liar? Let's do a little digging.

First, let's dig into the Bible.

Matthew 12:13–14
Who was conspiring in this passage? Why?

John 7:45–52
The Pharisees claimed that others were deceived by Jesus. But who was attempting a false arrest?

John 11:45–48
The Pharisees admit that Jesus performed signs. But why didn't they listen to Jesus?

There is evidence in the Talmud (nonbiblical Jewish writings) that Jewish authorities sought to arrest Jesus. Why? For one thing, "he has practiced sorcery" (Mishnah tractate, *Sanhedrin* 43a). In other words, they knew He had performed signs and miracles that pointed to Him as the Son of God. There are numerous times where the Pharisees tried to trick Jesus into a lie or a mistake, but they could never catch Him. They might be willing to conspire and lie, but Jesus was no liar.

Lunatic

If Jesus said He was the Son of God, and He was not a liar, then maybe He really believed it. Maybe He was crazy. That's another argument, anyway.

There's just one little thing. Jesus was willing to die. And so were His disciples. And still are, two thousand years later.

Read or listen to **Acts 5:27–40**.

What is Gamaliel's advice?

Yes, there are false prophets in this world. But very few are willing to die for their cause. And if they do, their followers usually forsake the cause soon after. But generation after generation, people still believe that Jesus is who He says He is. And they're still willing to die for that belief. Of all the other religions in the world, none of them proclaim that their leader died for them.

It's interesting to note that even Jesus' family thought He was crazy. The Gospels of Matthew, Mark, and Luke all record the time that Jesus' family came to Him, probably because they thought He'd lost His mind. We know later, however, that Mary believed, as did His brothers James and Jude.

30

Lord

If Jesus is not lying or crazy, He must truly be the Lord. And the triune God makes this clear as only God can. God's Word foretold Jesus' coming thousands of years before it happened. Let's take a look at just a few of those prophecies.

More than 500 years beforehand
Zechariah 9:9

More than 700 years beforehand
Micah 5:2

More than 700 years beforehand
Isaiah 9:6–7

About 1,000 years beforehand
Psalm 22:14–18

More than 700 years beforehand
Isaiah 53:3–12

Prophecies

There are literally hundreds of prophecies that were recorded centuries before Jesus came. And Jesus fulfilled them all. Could people have changed the Old Testament prophecies to fit Jesus' life? Well, in the late 1940s (as in after World War II, the age of planes and X-rays), a shepherd found the Dead Sea Scrolls hidden in a cave. We'll take a closer look at these later. But these scrolls were the Old Testament, sealed and hidden away, some from 300 or 400 years before Jesus was born. These scrolls match the Old Testament we have.

31

If time is short, encourage learners to dig deeper into these verses at home. This work could also be divided, having pairs or small groups each take a prophecy to explore. The key point is that there were clear prophecies about Jesus centuries before He was born. There are some brief videos online you can show that illustrate the incredible odds that Jesus was able to fulfill all of these prophecies.

Connections

In Jesus Christ

Billions of people over thousands of years have proclaimed Jesus as Lord. And despite differences, Christians (by definition) all believe in Christ. So who is Jesus? Here's what Christians through the centuries and all over the world proclaim in the Apostles' Creed:

I BELIEVE . . .

in Jesus Christ, His only Son, our Lord, who was conceived by the Holy Spirit, born of the Virgin Mary, suffered under Pontius Pilate, was crucified, died and was buried. He descended into hell. The third day He rose again from the dead. He ascended into heaven and sits at the right hand of God, the Father Almighty. From thence He will come to judge the living and the dead.

What Does This Mean?

This is only one part of the Creed, but there's so much to it! For now, take a look at **Questions 148–150** in *Luther's Small Catechism with Explanation*. See the Bible passages there? Jot down some of the references for the passages that were helpful for your learning about Jesus.

Make a Plan

We were able to see how Jesus must be Lord, but there is so much more to learn! Don't worry; we'll continue to dig deeper throughout this course. For now, however, write two important things you learned about Jesus today. Or, put another way, what would you say to a friend who thinks that Jesus is just a nice guy?

As we said earlier, Jesus is the only leader of a religion who died for His people. He's also the only one who rose from the dead. That sure supports the whole "Jesus is Lord" statement! But how can we be sure? We'll discuss that in the next lesson.

32

If your learners have already completed a thorough catechism study, this section may not be necessary at all. If not, this might become the core content of your lesson today, or even a bonus lesson. You can extend this learning by providing poster board for more writing space. If you just want learners to skim, you can direct them to read the answers to the Questions without digging into all the verses.

If writing is not a strength for learners and gets in the way of deeper thinking, have them tell you their responses and then write them in shortened form.

Check for Understanding

Before your learners leave, consider ways you can give them feedback for next week.

- **Exit Ticket:** As learners leave, ask each one to tell one truth about Jesus before they exit the door.
- **Video Witness:** Ask learners to pair up, recording a witness as to who Jesus is. They can share the video with you, which you will then send to the entire class and parents and caregivers.

Did Jesus Really Die and Rise Again?

Timeless Truth

Jesus lives and has redeemed me to be His own.

Lesson Focus

The learner will share evidence that the death and resurrection of Jesus were real events, witnessed by many people.

Allow time for learners to skim and review the crucifixion and resurrection accounts from Scripture and then summarize the key events in their own words. If your group is large, this could be done in small groups of two or three.

Or have learners tell you all that they know about the crucifixion and resurrection accounts, listing that information where all can see. Then, go to the Scriptures together to find what's missing.

8 Did Jesus Really Die and Rise Again?

Consider This

Skim and summarize the account of Jesus' death and resurrection from **Mark 15–16** and/or **John 18:1–20:18**.

I can share evidence that the death and resurrection of Jesus were real events, witnessed by many people.

33

Unit 2: Jesus

Jesus lives and has redeemed me to be His own.

Review the information from Lesson 6 as needed and then add the new facts concerning the crucifixion.

Help learners identify the problems with the anti-resurrection theories.

The Swoon Theory

- How could Jesus escape the tomb after the whipping and crucifixion He endured?
- How did Jesus evade the guards at the tomb?
- How did Jesus survive the spear wound that punctured His lung and heart?
- How did Jesus escape His tightly wound grave clothes?

The Theft Theory

- If the soldiers were sleeping, how would they know who stole the body?
- If the soldiers were sleeping on duty, wouldn't they have been punished?
- If the disciples stole Jesus' body, would they all have been willing to die for the lie?

Digging Deeper

Crucifixion Clues

In Lesson 6, you learned the importance of non-Christian witnesses to the facts of Christ's life. The Greek historian Tacitus reported the execution of Jesus by orders from the governor Pontius Pilate during the reign of Emperor Tiberius.

Thallus, another Classical historian, writes about a lengthy darkness during the time of Jesus' crucifixion. Luke also mentions this three-hour darkness in his Gospel (23:44–45).

Phlegon, a secular authority, attempts to explain the darkness during the crucifixion as a total eclipse that occurred during full moon at the time of Tiberius Caesar.

Lucian, a Greek satirist, labeled Christians "misguided creatures" who worshiped a crucified "sage."

The Anti-Resurrection Theories

Review each of the three theories that claim Jesus was not truly resurrected. What problems do you see with each theory?

The Swoon Theory

This theory claims Jesus simply fainted, revived in the tomb, and escaped, giving the appearance of being resurrected.

The Theft Theory

This theory claims that the disciples came and stole Jesus' body from the tomb. This theory is based in part on the claims of the tomb guards in **Matthew 28:13**.

The Hallucination Theory

This theory claims the disciples were all experiencing a mass hallucination when they claimed Jesus appeared to them following His crucifixion.

34

The Hallucination Theory

- Mass hallucinations of this kind and duration are unknown.
- Many people ate and drank with, touched, and interacted with the risen Jesus.

The Persecuted People

Historians Pliny the Younger and Tacitus reported the persecution and execution of Christ's followers in the first and second centuries. Romans developed many "creative" and gruesome methods of execution, including covering people in animal skins and having dogs tear them apart, nailing Christians to a cross, and turning Christians into human torches to illuminate nighttime festivals.

How might the willingness of believers to risk these punishments be seen as a proof of Jesus' resurrection?

Use online resources to explore how Christians around the world are suffering persecution for their beliefs. How could we assist these fellow believers?

Why is the reality of the resurrection essential to the Christian faith? See **1 Corinthians 15:3–28**.

35

Despite the constant threat to believers in the Early Church, they remained faithful, even to the point of death. If they knew the resurrection was false, why would they endure to the point of death?

Without the resurrection, our faith has no substance. Without Jesus' resurrection, we have no hope of our own resurrection.

These pages are for working through and talking about together, not for independent fill-in-the-blank exercises. If you want learners to interact with the text more closely, try pairing up learners to work together to read and answer the questions and then present their findings to the class.

Allow time for learners to develop a plan for sharing the information they learned in this lesson. If time is tight, they could complete this activity on their own at home.

Giving learners the opportunity to develop their plans verbally with you or as part of a group will help all learners process and organize their thoughts and learn from one another.

CONNECTIONS

MAKE A PLAN

Consider your friends or family who doubt the reality of Jesus' death and resurrection. Write a plan for how you could share with them some of the information you learned in this lesson. Remember that a gentle response works better than an attack of other people's unbelief.

36

CHECKS FOR UNDERSTANDING

Before your learners leave, consider ways you can give them feedback for next week.

- **Quiz Questions:** Have learners write a question that you will use to review at the beginning of your next session.
- **Learning Log:** Ask learners to write in their Learning Log one or two examples of how the Early Church proclaimed the truth of the resurrection.

When Will Jesus Return? Why Does His Return Matter?

Timeless Truth

Jesus lives and has redeemed me to be His own.

Lesson Focus

The learner will share with others ways that Jesus keeps His promises and how He will make all things new when He returns.

Before beginning this lesson, take a few moments to assess what learners already understand concerning the second coming of Christ.

9 When Will Jesus Return? Why Does His Return Matter?

Consider This

You're in a classroom, and your teacher tells you, "I need to take Sara to the office for a moment. Keep doing your homework; I'll be right back."

Do you believe he'll be right back?

You're at home, and your mom tells you, "I need to go grocery shopping. Finish cleaning your room; I'll be right back."

Do you believe she will be right back?

Jesus Says . . .

The past few lessons have been incredibly important. Let's recap:

- Jesus existed.
- Jesus is not crazy or a liar, so He is who He says He is: the Son of God, our Savior, our Lord.
- Jesus fulfilled all the prophecies about the Messiah, including dying and rising from the dead.
- In other words, we can trust Jesus. He keeps all His promises.

Because we can trust Jesus, who did everything He said He would (even rising from the dead), we can trust what He says about the triune God, about the Bible, about—well—everything.

So we'll be using His Word as truth throughout the course. And we'll also be using the other tools God has given us as we defend the faith. (See Lesson 5 for a recap.) But back to what Jesus says . . .

Jesus ascended into heaven, but before He left, He said the words recorded in **Matthew 28:18–20**. And when John had a vision about the future, recorded in Revelation, Jesus ended the whole Bible with the words recorded in **Revelation 22:18–20**. What did He say?

Think About It . . .

Do you believe Him? And if so, why does it matter?

I can share with others ways that Jesus keeps His promises and how He will make all things new when He returns.

JESUS LIVES AND HAS REDEEMED ME TO BE HIS OWN.

UNIT 2: JESUS 37

Decide how much background learners already have with this to see how deeply you need to dig into these questions. This could be a good time to divide into groups and have each group present on a designated Question.

Digging Deeper

While We Wait

Because Jesus has done absolutely everything He said He would do, we can believe that He will keep His promise to come back. We can also trust the prophecies He's given us.

So why does this matter?

Let's think back to the opening questions. Let's say your teacher came back, and no one was doing their homework. Or your mom came back from shopping, and your room was still a mess. What would happen?

What did Jesus tell us to do while we wait for His return? Review **Matthew 28:18–20**.

We have a job to do! While we wait, God has given us a purpose, a calling, a vocation. We are to share the truth of Jesus with others. What happens if we don't?

I'm Coming Back . . .

Because we know Jesus is coming back, we also know what will happen to us. Jesus died and rose. We will die, but we will also rise again. We will live forever with Jesus, body and soul.

Check out **Questions 223–225** in *Luther's Small Catechism with Explanation*. What phrases or Bible passages jump out at you?

38

Christians from all generations believed they were living in the last days. In **Mark 13:3–8**, Peter, James, John, and Andrew ask Jesus to tell them when the last days would be fulfilled. Jesus assured them that we will see signs of the End Times, but only the Father knows when the Last Day will come. "But concerning that day or that hour, no one knows, not even the angels in heaven, nor the Son, but only the Father" (Mark 13:32). As Christians, we live assured of the promise of heaven, which is ours through faith, but we need not worry about when the Last Day will come.

Be Prepared

Check out some of the things that Jesus said would happen in the last days, and jot them down. Circle the ones that have already happened.

Mark 13:1–8

1 Corinthians 15:51–52

1 Thessalonians 4:16

Isaiah 65:17–18

Revelation 7:9

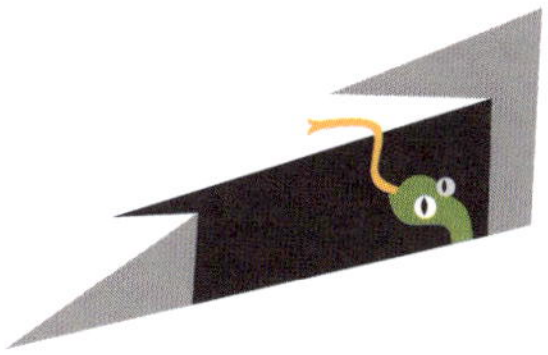

What hasn't happened yet? Since we can trust Jesus, we won't be surprised when these things come to pass. We will be prepared.

Be on Guard

As you saw in some of the prophecies above, there will be false prophets who claim to know when the world will end. This is a clear sign that those people are false. Read **Question 227** in *Luther's Small Catechism with Explanation*. Do we know when Jesus is coming back?

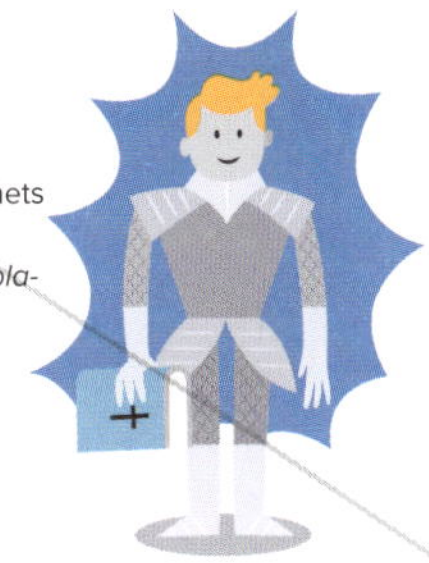

Rest Assured

No, we don't know the day or time. But we do know what is going to happen. And we also know what to look for. We also have hope. We don't have to worry about becoming a ghost. We don't even become angels or mere spiritual wisps floating around. (We'll talk about these things more in-depth later.) When we die, our spirit will rest with the Lord. And that's not all. We will rest assured in the promise that Jesus will come. And all things will be made new. Our bodies will be perfect. Nothing will hurt. All will be as it should be—forever.

Knowing the end, how does that impact how you view today?

39

Let learners use a Bible app to listen to or read these passages. Or give learners time (and maybe assistance) to find these passages in their Bibles and help them highlight them so they can use them again later in their lives.

Mark 13:1–8: Both. The temple was destroyed in AD 70; the rest will come one day.

1 Corinthians 15:51–52: To come.

1 Thessalonians 4:16: To come.

Isaiah 65:17–18: To come.

Revelation 7:9: Ongoing.

Do your learners need to get up and move around? Try this after you read the Bible passages. Draw a line in the middle of the board. Split your class into two teams, giving each one a half of the board. Set the timer and challenge them to write down as many end-time prophecies they can remember on their side of the board. This can help you see what points need more (or less) discussion. (Remind the learners that they won't want to shout out answers, so they'll have to take turns writing on the board.)

CONNECTIONS

MAKE A PLAN

Consider one of the following situations:

- A friend wonders if his grandma is an angel
- A cousin thinks she'll just disappear when she dies
- A neighbor wonders if the guy on the internet is right in his end-of-world prediction

Write what you can say. Remember to use love as you tell the truth in your response.

40

After some preliminary planning time, pair up learners to share. Then, challenge them to create a skit and role play. Students can learn from one another as they practice these dialogues.

CHECK FOR UNDERSTANDING

Before your learners leave, consider ways you can give them feedback for next week.

- **Role Play:** Use the optional activity in the margin as a way to assess learning: not only what learners know but also how they are practicing their apologetics strategies.
- **Big Questions:** This lesson probably sparked a number of new questions. If learners are asking these during class, encourage them to write them down. Take this time to invite more questions, collecting them so you can address them together as a class throughout the course.

Unit 3: Trusting God and His Word

Timeless Truth

Our loving God exists and gives us His living and active Word.

Essential Question

What do I need to know about God and His Word?

Focus Statements

10. The learner will explain some of the evidence that proves there is a God, including the fact that, in love, God gave His Word.
11. The learner will be able to explain that the Bible is completely the inspired Word of God and also refute some critics' claims that the Scriptures are filled with errors.
12. The learner will tell about how God gave His Word through the apostles, prophets, and others who wrote as the Holy Spirit led them.
13. The learner can point to the Creed as a summary of what God has done for His people and to the Bible as God's Word for salvation.

Assessment Options

1. **Preassessment Options**

   Before you begin this unit, have each learner spend a few minutes writing down or telling you or a partner personal responses to the following.

   - Who is God?
   - Why can I trust the Bible?
   - How does the Bible shape my worldview?

   After learners have finished, either collect the answers (to read and leave feedback) or quickly go over them together as a class. You'll get a sense of where each learner is coming from as you begin.

2. **Formative Assessment Options**

   Formative assessments are ways to monitor learning. Choose from the following:

   a. Learning Log: After each class, have learners write in their Learning Log one important thing they discovered in that class.

   b. Reflection Tools: As this is the third unit, your learners are likely familiar with these tools. Now, you can consider asking about the reflections themselves, using questions like these: What do you like most about these tools? How have you grown as a learner?

3. **Summative Assessment Options**

   Summative assessments evaluate learning at the end of an instructional unit. Choose from the following:

   a. Learning Portfolio: Have learners complete a variety of formative assessments over the course of this unit. At the end of the unit, they will compile at least one of each type of formative assessment, along with completed lesson notes and other samples you require. Learners who complete these tasks over the course of the unit will find them to be a great summative assessment. *Note*: At the beginning of the unit, provide a list of samples you will collect so there are no surprises at the end.

   b. Video Essay: Check for understanding by asking your learners to record themselves giving short answers to several questions. This could be done inside or outside of class, using various mobile devices. You could ask learners to pair up as they help each other record. This will also give them practice articulating their faith in front of a peer.

   You may write your own questions, or use the following questions based on the unit:

- How would you describe God?
- Who is the authority on who God is?
- What is it that all Christians have believed for thousands of years?

Teaching Tips

1. This unit is the clincher in terms of preparing the learners to exist within the Christian worldview. Once the Word of God and God Himself are established as real, trustworthy sources of wisdom and knowledge, these facts can be used to defend the faith with others who have been familiarized with that worldview. Christians themselves have questions, so this unit reminds believers that God's Word is in fact true and that it can be used in future lessons regarding a variety of issues.
2. Remember that your learners will vary in their learning from topic to topic. Most likely, you are teaching this course to learners who have already gone through a catechism study. If not, you'll need to work through more foundational knowledge from time to time. Other times, a lesson might revisit something learners know well but may still challenge them, as the lessons in this course come from an angle of articulating the faith to others. That said, there will be times when the learners themselves will need some convincing. In other words, it's critical that you use your discretion to pick and choose the parts of the lessons you want to spend time on, based on your learners' prior knowledge. Remember, you are aiming for learning. Always ask yourself: Do my learners better understand the content of the Timeless Truth and the Lesson Focus? How do I know? Keep returning to this.
3. At the beginning of each lesson, consider giving some form of preassessment to help you make decisions regarding the lesson depth as well as to help you note the learning that occurred during the lesson.
4. Again, this entire curriculum uses the 2017 edition of *Luther's Small Catechism with Explanation*. The references to the Questions will match only with that edition. It's a good idea to keep several on hand for learners to use as needed in the lessons.

Color Key for Teacher Notes

Tan = Specific additional assessments

Blue = Extra activities or questions

Green = Educational tips and directions for specific activities

Gold = Explanations of theological concepts or background for the teacher

How Do We Know There Is a God?

Timeless Truth

Our loving God exists and gives us His living and active Word.

Lesson Focus

The learner will explain some of the evidence that proves there is a God, including the fact that, in love, God gave His Word.

Take some time to recap what you've learned so far: What do we know about Jesus? What can we be sure about? It is no mistake that one of the first lessons addressed the authenticity of Jesus. He speaks as an authority on so much that it makes sense to begin with His credibility. Also, it's a good reminder as to why worldview is so important. "Because the Bible says so" is often our first line of defense when talking to others. But if they don't trust the Bible in their worldview, we need to back up and start with more foundational truths.

10 How Do We Know There Is a God?

Consider This

Christians (and even many non-Christians) believe that there is a God. However, there is a growing number of people who don't want to believe that there is a God at all. Think about your own life. What about your world and daily life lead you to believe that there is a God?

Knowing God

So let's think about this using some logic.

If God exists, and He made all that we see, He must be powerful. If He's not loving, we probably are sunk no matter what; it's not important whether we know Him. But why are there so many wonderful things if He isn't loving?

If He's a loving God, He probably wants us to know about Him. So how would He tell us about Him? He'd probably give us blessings. And He'd probably care for us. He would want to talk with us. He would want us to know that He loves us.

What kinds of blessings do you see in this world?

In what kinds of ways does God talk to us?

This question may be too big to process immediately, so give it a little time. You can start with smaller questions. "What things in your life make you think, 'Wow, we have a great God'?" You may have learners who point straight to their faith or to church. Allow the brainstorm to continue; this question gets further clarified in the next few activities.

Think About It . . .

If God doesn't exist, what happened before time began?

I can explain some of the evidence that proves there is a God, including the fact that, in love, God gave His Word.

Unit 3: Trusting God and His Word

Our Loving God Exists and Gives Us His Living and Active Word.

41

The universe is an incredible piece of evidence for a God, but of course this has been called into question. Try not to dwell too much of the origin of creation today, if at all possible. Make sure learners know that it will come up later on in the course (particularly after the authenticity of the Bible is established).

In order to reduce frustration around finding questions in Luther's Small Catechism, have at least one copy bookmarked and ready to go for this question. If you're comfortable with doing so, highlight the question that will be talked about today and hand it to learners to read or to help them find the same question in their own catechism.

If you have a teaching space with a digital projector, project this question on the wall for all to look at together.

Digging Deeper

Natural Knowledge of God

Deep down, humans know that there is a God. Sure, we can fight against it or ignore it, but God gave us a natural knowledge of Him. Here are ways we know about Him even if we've never been taught anything.

The Heavens Declare

Read or listen to **Question 105** and its Bible verses in *Luther's Small Catechism with Explanation*.

Think about your world. What things show God's goodness? His power?

Later on in this course, we will talk about other theories of how the world could have been made without a God. Spoiler alert: Evolution can't explain what started the Big Bang or how nonliving things became living. No one has an answer for that. Also, many scientists are Christian. Their studies complement their faith and point them to a loving, orderly God.

Written on Our Hearts

Even people who don't believe in any God talk about morality or right and wrong. They might even talk about a conscience. Their sense of right and wrong might be cloudy, but people tend to universally agree on many rights and wrongs. Or they at least agree that there is a right and wrong (especially if they've been wronged!). What are examples of things that most people seem to agree are right and wrong?

42

Most likely, examples will coincide with the commandments that pertain to our neighbor. However, there are some truths that society has put further into question. For example, most people will agree that murder is wrong. But the world sometimes condones abortion and euthanasia. Most will agree that stealing is wrong but probably feel that it's okay to download or share a copyrighted digital file. Sexual morality is particularly under attack, and your own learners may be surprised at God's will for sexual purity.

The Revealed Knowledge of God

If we only needed to know God existed, He might not spend much time worrying about revealing Himself to us. But there are essential things He wants us to know. Consider, for example, the following.

1. He loves us.
2. He made a perfect world, but Satan tempted Adam and Eve, bringing sin into the world.
3. Because of sin, bad things happen. People die. And worse yet, our sin separates us from God forever. (Because of sin, not everyone realizes or cares that God exists.)
4. He loves us so much that He sent His Son, Jesus, to become a man, die, and rise in our place. Justice has been served to pay the price, so we are set free from sin, death, and the devil.
5. Those who believe in Jesus will be saved.

Jesus died and rose again as He promised. Because He kept His promises, we can trust the truthfulness of the rest of the Scriptures.

God's Word

We've talked before about the power of God's Word. Let's review some ways God uses His Word to reveal Himself to us.

God's Word creates.
God spoke into being His creation, which reveals God Himself through natural knowledge. But that was the last page, so let's move on.

God's Word speaks to people directly.
There have been times in the past where God spoke directly to someone. Adam, Eve, Abram, Moses, Samuel, and many others have had conversations with God.

God's Word speaks to people through people.
God uses prophets to speak to others. He uses pastors to speak to others. He even uses us to speak to others.

God's Word became flesh and dwelt among us.
We are saved by the Word, that is, Jesus Himself.

God's Word has been recorded and handed down.
When we have questions about God, we can go to His Word and find the same answers that all believers have found for generations. We might take it for granted, but to have God's Word in our hands is an incredible gift from God.

It makes sense, right? If there is a God, and if He is a loving God, He will make sure we know about Him and His love and the way we can be with Him forever.

43

There is a lot of content and print on this page! Having more information than activities can be confusing or overwhelming for some learners. Help them stay focused by asking them to highlight key words or to create a picture that illustrates a particular point. Small groups could present each point, creating a mini poster on printer paper. Post all pages somewhere to create the "big picture."

Read, or have learners take turns reading, the information on this page. After each point, stop and ask for someone to use his or her own words to repeat what was read. Repetition makes the content real for learners, and it allows you to assess their understanding.

For learners who are overwhelmed by the amount of print on this page, help them use two pieces of paper or note cards to block off the part of the page that they aren't reading and make a frame around the piece that they need to focus on. Read aloud portions as needed, in small chunks of content rather than all at once.

Have Scripture passages bookmarked and highlighted in a Bible or two for quicker access. Or help learners practice using a Bible app to find and listen to these passages.

Answering these questions in writing takes some higher-order thinking to synthesize the content from this lesson and get it down on paper. For more concrete learners and learners who take a little more time to process information, have them talk through their answers before they try to put it into writing, doing one question at a time.

Option: Have pairs or small groups each talk about a different question to summarize their thoughts and then respond in writing or by speaking to the whole class.

CONNECTIONS

TRULY, TRULY

We've established that Jesus has a track record of being perfectly reliable. What does He say about God? Read a few examples and share.

John 3:16

John 5:19

John 8:58

John 13:20

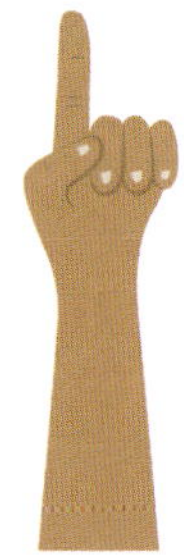

SUM IT UP

Wow! There has been a lot of material to sift through in this lesson. Now, put it into your words.

- How do we know there is a God?
- What kind of evidence is there outside of the Scriptures?
- Why would God give us His Word?

44

CHECKS FOR UNDERSTANDING

Before your learners leave, consider ways you can give them feedback for next week.

- **Sum It Up:** Use the "Sum It Up" section today to see how learners were able to summarize their learning.
- **Learning Log**: Ask learners to answer one or both of the following questions: How do I know that God exists? How do I know that God loves me?

How Do We Know the Bible Is True?

Timeless Truth

Our loving God exists and gives us His living and active Word.

Lesson Focus

The learner will be able to explain that the Bible is completely the inspired Word of God and also refute some critics' claims that the Scriptures are filled with errors.

11 How Do We Know the Bible Is True?

Consider This

Early documents were not written on paper. In fact, paper wasn't invented until about 100 BC in China during the Han Dynasty. Ts'ai Lun, a government official, discovered that mixing mulberry bark and hemp rags with water and then drying the mixture in the sun produced a form of paper.

Before the invention of paper, written documents took different forms. Match the writing surfaces to the descriptions below:

Papyrus **Parchment** **Vellum** **Cuneiform**

__________________ characters made with a reed on a clay or wax tablet were first used in Sumeria and Mesopotamia as early as 3500 BC.

__________________ is a paperlike material made in ancient Egypt from flattened reed stems laid at right angles and pounded flat.

__________________ is a thin layer of untanned sheep or goat skin used as a writing surface; named after the city of Pergamon in ancient Greece, which specialized in its production.

__________________ is thin calfskin, and is considered the highest-quality writing surface; its Latin name is *vitulinum*, which means "made from calf."

I can explain that the Bible is completely the inspired Word of God and also refute some critics' claims that the Scriptures are filled with errors.

Unit 3: Trusting God and His Word — Our loving God exists and gives us His living and active Word.

45

Early paper, and the writing surfaces that predated it, was very fragile. As a result, manuscripts required constant maintenance and copying. We'll talk more about this process throughout this lesson.

Cuneiform characters made with a reed on a clay or wax tablet were first used in Sumeria and Mesopotamia as early as 3500 BC.

Papyrus is a paper-like material made in ancient Egypt from flattened reed stems laid at right angles and pounded flat.

Parchment is a thin layer of untanned sheep or goat skin used as a writing surface; it is named after the city of Pergamon in ancient Greece, which specialized in its production.

Vellum is thin calfskin, and considered the highest quality writing surface; its Latin name is *vitulinum*, which means "made from calf."

If you have learners who aren't particularly strong readers, read this section aloud or do it together as a group.

If copying the words into small spaces is a struggle, let learners draw a line. The point is to learn about the different kinds of writing materials, not how well your learners can write.

Review together the facts about the various manuscripts of the New Testament. This section isn't meant to be read independently.

Ask volunteers to read, but never put learners on the spot to do so.

The number of biblical manuscripts and the relatively short time between the events and the manuscript help assure us of the accuracy of the biblical text.

Point out that few people question the accuracy of Homer's history or if Sophocles really wrote *Oedipus the King*. Yet their works have greater gaps than the biblical manuscripts.

We can trust the Bible because God assures us of the accuracy of His Word.

Option: If you have time and learners are interested, have them do some online research in class about some of the items mentioned in this list.

Digging Deeper

Major Manuscripts

How do the earliest copies of the Bible compare with other ancient writings? How can we trust the Bible writers?

- When the Masoretes copied biblical texts, they wrote only one line at a time. Then, they counted the letters and spaces. If there was an error, the copy was destroyed.
- The Dead Sea Scroll of Isaiah dates to 100 BC and is 95 percent identical in a word-for-word comparison with other manuscripts (the few discrepancies are minor).
- There are 24,000 early copies of the New Testament, but only 643 copies of Homer's *The Iliad*.
- The time between the completion of the New Testament and the earliest known copy of it is 225 years. For *The Iliad*, the gap is 400 years.
- The earliest known manuscripts of *Oedipus the King* by Sophocles were written more than 1,400 years after his death.
- The Cyrus Cylinder, a clay barrel covered with writing that was created in 539 BC, was unearthed by archaeologists during the excavation of Babylon in 1879. The cylinder verifies both Isaiah's prophecy naming Cyrus and the events in 2 Chronicles concerning the resettlement of Jerusalem, following the exile.

We believe the Word of God has the power in itself to convince readers and hearers of its authority. Because it is God's Word, it is self-authenticating. The Word of God does what it says.

Confidence

In the Gospel, the central message of the Bible, God promises us new life on the basis of the life, death, and resurrection of Jesus. God's promises alone create faith in Jesus Christ. Jesus Himself, whom we trust, declares that all the Scriptures are God's own words, completely dependable in all they teach, and without error.

Read **Question 8** in your catechism and summarize the three reasons we can have confidence in the truth of God's Word.

47

8. Why can we be confident that the Bible is the authoritative and inerrant Word of God?

A. Jesus uses the Old Testament Scriptures as God's Word. He continually affirms Scripture as authoritative with phrases such as "It is written" and "Have you not read?" (Matthew 4:4, 7, 10; 19:4). He assures us that "Scripture cannot be broken" (John 10:35).

B. Jesus claims the same authority for Himself, saying for example, "I say to you" (Matthew 5:22, 28, 32), or "Truly, truly, I say" (John 6:47; see also 5:47), or explicitly claiming His words to be "spirit and life" (John 6:63; see also John 8:31–32).

C. Just as God called and authorized prophets in the Old Testament, put His words in their mouths, and fulfilled their prophecies, so also Jesus called and authorized His apostolic witnesses to speak His Word, guided by His Spirit (Luke 10:16; John 14:26; Acts 1:8; 2 Peter 1:16–21; 1 John 1:1–4).

Your group may include learners with a wide variety of both academic skills and catechism knowledge. Be careful about assuming that all learners will be able to read and summarize independently. Working in pairs or small groups can help alleviate stress for learners in this regard.

9. Do we use human reason to understand the Bible?

Yes, but human reason must be used within appropriate limits, as a servant of the text. To understand the Bible's meaning properly, the guidance of the Holy Spirit is essential.

A. Because Scripture is given in human language, to read and rightly understand what it says, we must humbly use human reason in such matters as context, grammar, and logic.

B. Because the Bible is God's Word and, unlike all other books, is inspired and inerrant, it is wrong to use human reason to question or deny its truthfulness. . . .

The Bible's truthfulness should not be questioned or denied (as happens, for example, with historical criticism).

CONNECTIONS

HUMAN (WITHOUT) REASON

Question 9 in the Small Catechism asks, "Do we use human reason to understand the Bible?" Read or listen to each of the suggested Bible verses and summarize what the Scriptures say about the use of human reason.

Psalm 119:73

Matthew 22:37

Acts 17:11

Romans 3:4

2 Corinthians 10:5

Colossians 2:8

2 Timothy 4:3–4

2 Peter 3:15–16

48

CHECKS FOR UNDERSTANDING

Before your learners leave, consider ways you can give them feedback for next week.

- **Create:** Use an online resource to help learners write their name in Greek letters. For extra fun, use brown craft paper that has been crumpled and flattened to look like parchment.
- **Learning Log:** In their Learning Log, have learners write one question they still have about the Bible.

How Did the Bible Come to Be?

Timeless Truth

Our loving God exists and gives us His living and active Word.

Lesson Focus

The learner will tell about how God gave His Word through the apostles, prophets, and others who wrote as the Holy Spirit led them.

Through the years, God led a series of authors to write the words that have become the accepted books of Scripture.

God's Word has two distinct sections, the Old Testament and the New Testament. Each of these testaments has its own important function. The Scripture verses at the bottom remind us that the Word was inspired through the work of the Holy Spirit.

Learners may have questions about the wide variety of English-language Bible translations. This curriculum is written using the English Standard Version, a very accurate translation of the original Hebrew, Greek, and Aramaic texts.

Option: Have learners list different Bible translations they have heard about. Help learners understand the difference between a Bible translation and a Bible paraphrase (a literal word-by-word review as opposed to a restatement of the text in different words). Use online resources to compare the differences in translations.

12 How Did the Bible Come to Be?

Consider This

Building a Canon

When we talk about building a canon, we're not talking about assembling a weapon used to launch projectiles at the enemy (that kind is spelled *cannon*). The *canon* we are talking about is an accepted list of books with authority. The biblical canon was not selected by a committee or an emperor. Rather, the Holy Spirit led Moses to begin writing around 1400 BC, and the books of the prophets were added as they received messages from God.

The Word

When reading God's Word, it's important to remember the two big divisions of the Bible: the Old Testament and the New Testament. The Bible is a sort of library of sixty-six books written over 1,500 years. The Old Testament includes thirty-nine books, all written before Jesus' birth; the New Testament is made of twenty-seven books that were written after Jesus' birth. Both testaments are super important, and they each play an important role in reading God's Word.

Think About It . . .

What do the two verses below tell you about how the Bible text came into existence?

Long ago, at many times and in many ways, God spoke to our fathers by the prophets, but in these last days He has spoken to us by His Son, whom He appointed the heir of all things, through whom also He created the world.

Hebrews 1:1–2

All Scripture is breathed out by God and profitable for teaching, for reproof, for correction, and for training in righteousness, that the man of God may be competent, equipped for every good work.

2 Timothy 3:16–17

Unit 3: Trusting God and His Word

Our loving God exists and gives us His living and active Word.

I can tell about how God gave His Word through the apostles, prophets, and others who wrote as the Holy Spirit led them.

49

Some people question the truth of the Old Testament because of the amazing and miraculous ways God worked on behalf of His people. While some of the events of the Old Testament have yet to be verified, ongoing archaeological studies continue to verify the biblical canon.

Explore resources available from reliable and scientific resources such as the Creation Museum, Ark Encounter, and the Museum of the Bible.

The pages of this lesson contain quite a bit of print. It is not intended for the learners to read all this independently. As leader, you can read the sections aloud or put it into your own words. Another option is to have learners read it together in smaller groups or pairs.

Never put learners on the spot to read in front of the class. Always ask for volunteers. Learners who are embarrassed about their reading skills are certainly not thinking about the content of the lesson.

Digging Deeper

Old Testament

The thirty-nine Old Testament books, from Genesis to Malachi, represent the known canon in the fourth century BC, long before Jesus walked on this earth. The Jews were convinced that the prophets had ceased to speak, so with no further word from God, their Scriptures were complete.

Though arranged in a different order, these books of history, poetry, and prophecy are the same ones Jesus Himself accepted. Throughout His ministry, Jesus referred to the Old Testament, even quoting the words of the prophets concerning Himself. Jesus clearly recognized the authenticity and authority of the Old Testament.

Think About It . . .

What reasons might someone give for doubting the authenticity of the Old Testament? What evidence could you share to support the truth of the Old Testament?

Books of the Old Testament

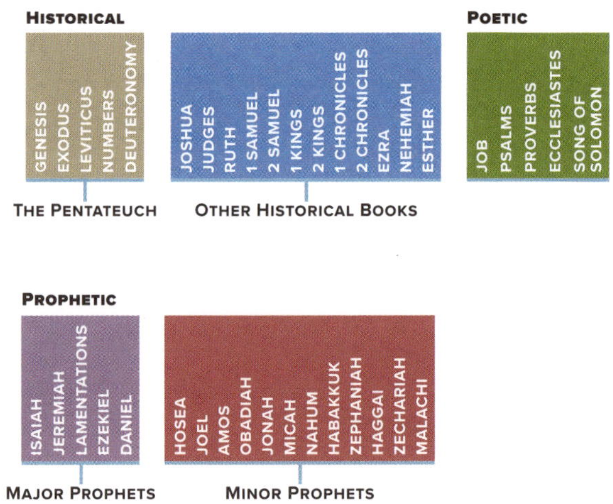

50

New Testament

As He prepares to ascend to heaven, Jesus commissions His followers to spread the Good News to all the earth as they teach everything they learned from Him. As a result, the Early Church gathered the writings of the apostles. The four Gospels, the Book of Acts, the thirteen letters of Paul, 1 Peter, and 1 John were all written by, or at the direction of, the apostles, so no one questioned their inclusion in the New Testament canon.

However, seven books were questioned: Hebrews, James, 2 Peter, 2 John, 3 John, Jude, and Revelation. The primary issue was the authorship of these books. The author of Hebrews is not named, but the contents of the book agree with the rest of Scripture, so it was included. James and Jude were written by Jesus' half brothers, so they were included. The style of 2 Peter varies from 1 Peter, but further study showed that although 1 Peter was written with the help of Silvanus, Peter wrote the second epistle on his own. The two short letters of 2 John and 3 John were written by "the Elder," and the style of language matches John's first letter. The Book of Revelation tells us it was written by "John," though some question whether this refers to the apostle.

By AD 350, the Bible as we know it, from Genesis through Revelation, was complete. Some Bibles today contain the Apocrypha, which was added by the Roman Catholic Church in 1546. These books were not part of the early canon, and they are never quoted by Jesus or early Jewish historians like Josephus and Philo.

> The central focus of all of the Scriptures, both Old and New Testament, is Jesus Christ. The Old Testament points forward to His coming, while the New Testament tells us of His work here on earth. Most important, the New Testament shows us how He lived a perfect life, suffered, died sacrificially, and was raised again to save us from our sins.

Think About It . . .

How does Paul's direction that the apostles and prophets serve as the foundation for God's Word help us identify the appropriate content for the biblical canon?

So then you are no longer strangers and aliens, but you are fellow citizens with the saints and members of the household of God, built on the foundation of the apostles and prophets, Christ Jesus Himself being the cornerstone.
Ephesians 2:19–20

> If you have a place to write on a white board or piece of poster paper, summarize this information in some lists where learners can see and follow this content in a visual format.

Books of the New Testament

Historical
Matthew
Mark
Luke
John
Acts

Epistles
Romans
1 Corinthians
2 Corinthians
Galatians
Ephesians
Philippians
Colossians
1 Thessalonians
2 Thessalonians
1 Timothy
2 Timothy
Titus
Philemon
Hebrews
James
1 Peter
2 Peter
1 John
2 John
3 John
Jude

Prophetic
Revelation

51

The Scriptures are completely inerrant, not even capable of error. Likewise, they are infallible, not capable of making a mistake. These facts are vital because it means we can completely trust the contents of the Bible. Our faith has a solid foundation, since it is built on the Scriptures.

CONNECTIONS

THE B-I-B-L-E

The Bible gathers together the writings of God's chosen prophets and apostles over a period of more than 1,500 years. Through the Holy Spirit, God Himself gave these writers the thoughts and words they recorded (verbal inspiration); such it is that the Bible is God's Word. Holy Scripture is therefore entirely reliable and gives us everything we need to know and believe for Christian faith and life.

Why is it important that the Bible is infallible? (incapable of making an error)

Why is it important that the Bible is inerrant? (without error)

For no prophecy was ever produced by the will of man, but men spoke from God as they were carried along by the Holy Spirit.
2 Peter 1:21

52

CHECKS FOR UNDERSTANDING

Before your learners leave, consider ways you can give them feedback for next week.

- **Quiz Questions:** Have learners write questions about this lesson and then pair up and ask each other their questions.
- **Learning Log:** In their Learning Log, have learners write down their favorite Bible book. Why is that particular book their favorite?

What Do We Know about Who God Is?

Timeless Truth

Our loving God exists and gives us His living and active Word.

Lesson Focus

The learner can point to the Creed as a summary of what God has done for His people and to the Bible as God's Word for salvation.

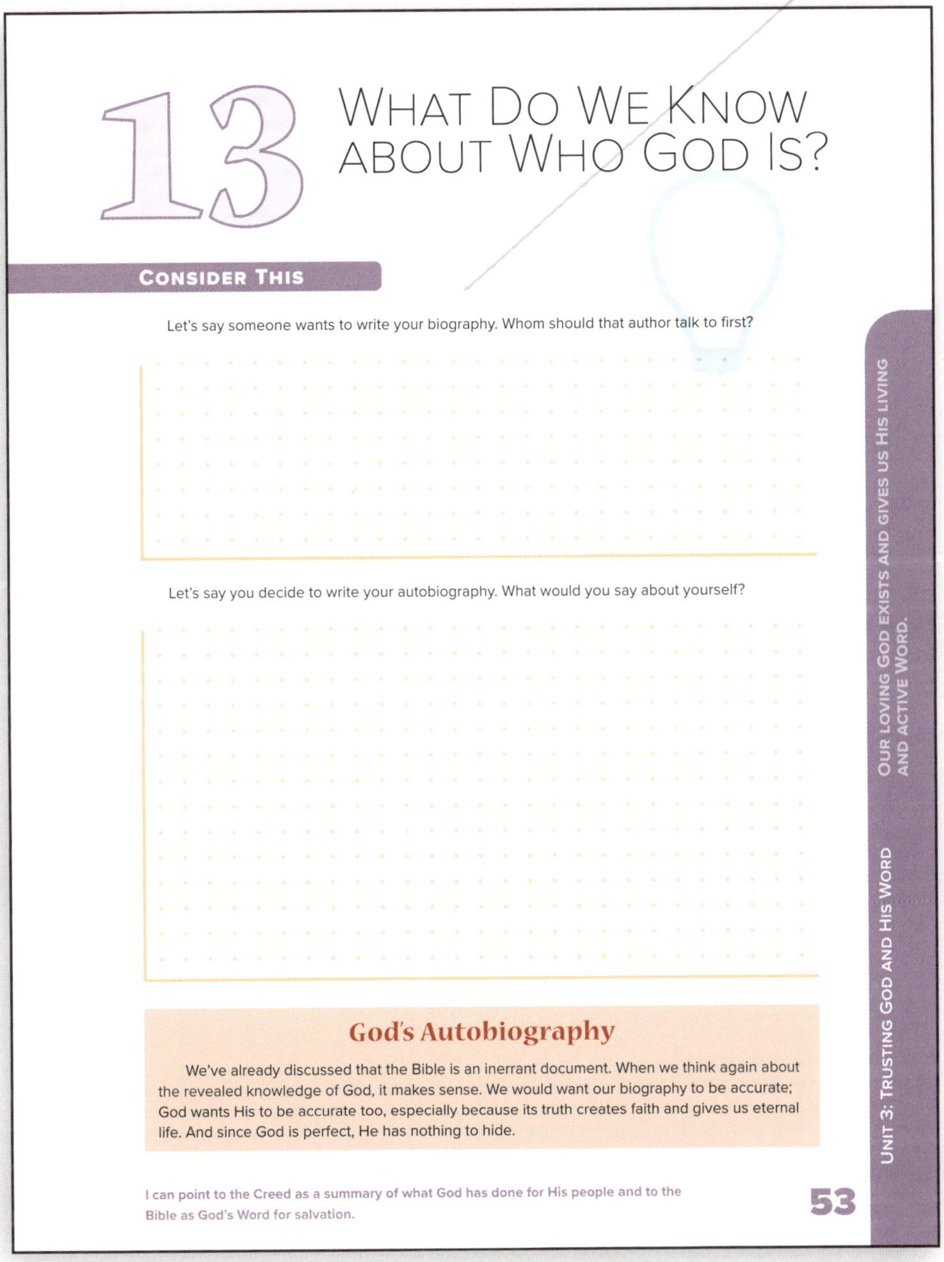

13 What Do We Know about Who God Is?

Consider This

Let's say someone wants to write your biography. Whom should that author talk to first?

Let's say you decide to write your autobiography. What would you say about yourself?

God's Autobiography

We've already discussed that the Bible is an inerrant document. When we think again about the revealed knowledge of God, it makes sense. We would want our biography to be accurate; God wants His to be accurate too, especially because its truth creates faith and gives us eternal life. And since God is perfect, He has nothing to hide.

I can point to the Creed as a summary of what God has done for His people and to the Bible as God's Word for salvation.

53

Unit 3: Trusting God and His Word

Our loving God exists and gives us His living and active Word.

These activities could be a great way to start the class, but be careful with learners who don't seem comfortable talking about themselves. Start with a learner who is more confident, if you ask for volunteers to share. Also make the point that while we might not always be reliable when talking about ourselves, God always is. We are sinful and sometimes try to hide who we are. God is holy and always wants us to know exactly who He is.

Most likely, your learners have already gone through a catechism study course, so this page will serve as a brief review. If not, this lesson may be most helpful if you spread it over a few class periods, walking through the Apostles' Creed in the Small Catechism.

This is a great activity to do in smaller groups, giving each group one section of the creed to discuss and present to the class. If you have a large enough group, have some groups work on the same sections.

DIGGING DEEPER

WHAT DOES THE BIBLE TELL US ABOUT GOD?

If we were to write down everything we know about God right here, it would be, well, as long as the Bible. That's going to take a while! So we're going to summarize what we know about God in two different ways.

THE CREED

We've talked about the Creed before. And if you've already studied the Small Catechism, you know it has a lot to say! It's likely that you say one of the three Christian creeds at church every week. But it never hurts to review!

Here is the Apostles' Creed, which all Christians have believed for centuries. It serves as a summary of what we know from the Bible.

> I believe in God, the Father Almighty, Maker of heaven and earth.
>
> And in Jesus Christ, His only Son, our Lord, who was conceived by the Holy Spirit, born of the Virgin Mary, suffered under Pontius Pilate, was crucified, died and was buried. He descended into hell. The third day He rose again from the dead. He ascended into heaven and sits at the right hand of God, the Father Almighty. From thence He will come to judge the living and the dead.
>
> I believe in the Holy Spirit, the holy Christian church, the communion of saints, the forgiveness of sins, the resurrection of the body, and the life everlasting. Amen.

What do we know about God the Father? You may want to look at the "What Does This Mean?" section for the First Article in the Small Catechism.

What do we know about God the Son? You may want to look at the "What Does This Mean?" section for the Second Article in the Small Catechism.

What do we know about God the Holy Spirit? You may want to look at the "What Does This Mean?" section for the Third Article in the Small Catechism.

What other thoughts come to mind when you think about the question "Who is God?"

54

The Salvation Summary

When Jesus talks about God's Word, He says this:

> *You search the Scriptures because you think that in them you have eternal life; and it is they that bear witness about Me.* John 5:39

Again, if our loving God wants to take the time to tell us something, He'll spend time making sure we know how we can be with Him forever and ever and ever (and ever . . .).

What is the way to eternal life?

> *Jesus said to him, "I am the way, and the truth, and the life. No one comes to the Father except through Me."* John 14:6

The way to eternal life is Jesus. As soon as Adam and Eve needed a Savior, God promised one. And the entire Old Testament anticipates the coming Savior. The entire New Testament demonstrates the Savior who has come (and who will come again). That's truly epic. Many Christians, therefore, highlight key parts of the Bible that point to the only way to heaven. In learning who God is, we learn what God has done for us to give us eternal life. Take some time to put these important points in the story of salvation into your own words.

Genesis 1:1

Genesis 3:15

Isaiah 11:1–2

Hosea 11:1

Luke 2

John 3:16

Matthew 28:18–20

Romans 3:23

Romans 6:23

Revelation 22:18–20

55

Option: Make this interactive! Set up stations ahead of time, planting these Bible verses in various places in the building. Walk together to each station, and ask volunteers to read the passage. Discuss out loud the message of each passage, and recap when you return to your classroom.

Have a Bible bookmarked and highlighted before class begins. Help learners, as needed, to find these in their own Bibles and highlight them. If you and your learners are all using *The Lutheran Study Bible*, the page numbers will be the same regardless of which version of *TLSB* you have.

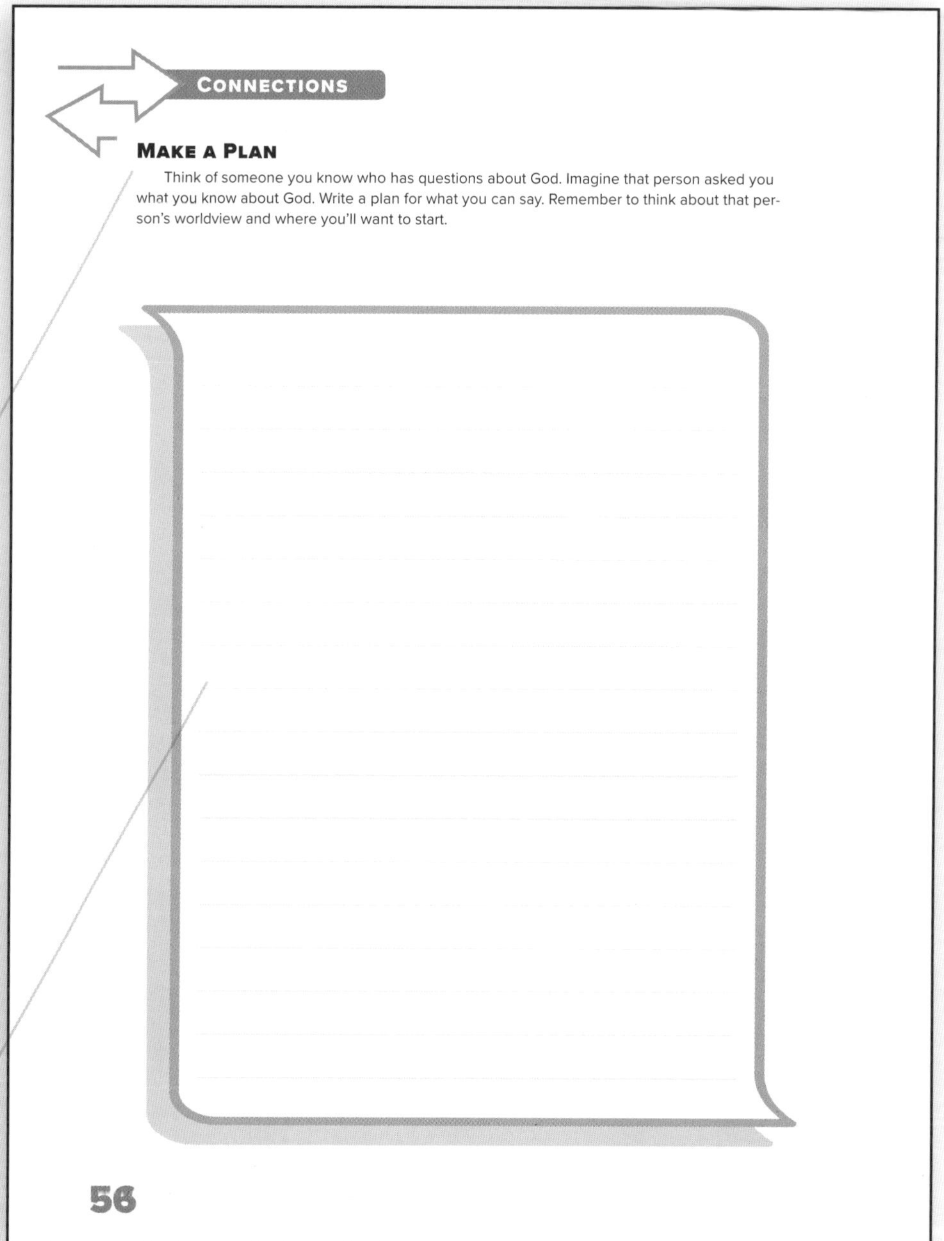

CONNECTIONS

MAKE A PLAN

Think of someone you know who has questions about God. Imagine that person asked you what you know about God. Write a plan for what you can say. Remember to think about that person's worldview and where you'll want to start.

56

Do learners need a prompt? Ask, "What is the most important thing to know about God?" This may spark a brainstorm session, which you could record on the white board or something similar to help get this writing time started.

For learners who struggle to get their thoughts down in writing, have them tell you their response; then, you write it and let them copy, or allow them to record their answer in a digital format.

CHECKS FOR UNDERSTANDING

Before your learners leave, consider ways you can give them feedback for next week.

- **Paired Discussion:** Ask learners to write down the answer to the question, "Who is God?" Then, invite them to share with a partner, practicing a witness of faith.
- **Dig Deeper:** There are many creative ways that Christians have summarized their faith in God over video and other means. Before class, find and preview a few examples. Play one or two at the end of class and ask learners to respond.

Unit 4: Beginnings

Timeless Truth

God created the heavens and the earth, He has redeemed His creation, and He will restore it.

Essential Question

Does it matter that I believe the Bible regarding the creation of all things?

Focus Statements

14. The learner will be able to explain that God created the universe in six days.
15. The learner will share that the world was created by God, not a chance product of evolution.
16. The learner will explain that the first chapters of Genesis lay a foundation for fundamental teachings of the faith.
17. The learner will tell how, through a worldwide flood, God cleansed the earth and saved Noah and his family.
18. The learner will be able to explain that God is the same yesterday, today, and forever.

Assessment Options

1. **Preassessment Options**

   Before you begin this unit, have each learner spend a few minutes writing down or telling you or a partner personal responses to the following:

   - How did this world come to be?
   - How does an understanding of Genesis impact your worldview?
   - Does God change?

   After learners have finished, either collect the answers (to read and leave feedback) or quickly go over them together as a class. Be careful not to put anyone on the spot, especially if you feel an answer isn't what you would like it to be. It's important that your learners trust you to keep their answers confidential. Reading or listening to these responses will give you a sense of where each learner is coming from as you begin.

2. **Formative Assessment Options**

   Formative assessments are ways to monitor learning. Choose from the following:

   a. Learning Log: After each class, have learners write in their Learning Log one important thing they discovered in that class.

   b. Reflection Tools: Your learners are likely familiar with these tools by now. Consider asking reflection questions about the reflection tools themselves: What do you like most about these tools? How have you grown as a learner?

3. **Summative Assessment Options**

   Summative assessments evaluate learning at the end of an instructional unit. Choose from the following:

   a. Learning Portfolio: Have learners complete a variety of formative assessments over the course of this unit. At the end of the unit, they will compile at least one of each type of formative assessment, along with completed lesson notes and other samples you require. Learners who complete these tasks over the course of the unit will find them to be a great summative assessment. *Note*: At the beginning of the unit, provide a list of samples you will collect so there are no surprises at the end.

   b. Video Essay: Check for understanding by asking your learners to record themselves giving short answers to several questions. This could be done inside or outside of class, using various mobile devices. You could ask learners to pair up as they help each other record. This will also give them practice articulating their faith in front of a peer.

You may write your own questions or use the following questions based on the unit:

- How does a Christian respond to those who believe that God did not create the heavens and the earth?
- What do the first chapters of Genesis say about our God?
- What evidence points to accounts such as the flood?

Teaching Tips

1. This unit may be highly anticipated by your learners. Some learners may be eager to gain support and tools to support the creation account. Others may be shocked, fully believing that Christians can believe in evolution. Demonstrate the same care in teaching as you would hope your learners will exhibit when defending the faith to others. There may be moments of exasperation from learners when they see logical fallacies in societal views on the origin of all things. Provide a safe place where learners can express their concerns and questions as you also maintain a spirit of love for those who need to hear the truth in love, both inside and outside of the classroom. Christians often experience disrespect in such conversations, and we can be tempted to retaliate. Pray for patience.
2. Remember that your learners will vary in their learning from topic to topic. Most likely, you are teaching this course to learners who have already gone through a catechism study. If not, you'll need to work through more foundational knowledge from time to time. Other times, a lesson might revisit something learners know well but may still challenge them, as the lessons in this course come from an angle of articulating the faith to others. That said, there will be times when the learners themselves will need some convincing. In other words, it's critical that you use your discretion to pick and choose the parts of each lesson you want to spend time on, based on your learners' prior knowledge. Remember, you are aiming for learning. Ask yourself: Do my learners better understand the content of the Timeless Truth and the Lesson Focus? How do I know? Keep returning to this.
3. At the beginning of each lesson, consider giving some form of preassessment to help you make decisions regarding the lesson depth and to help you note the learning that occurred during the lesson.
4. Again, this entire curriculum uses the 2017 edition of *Luther's Small Catechism with Explanation*. The references to the Questions will match only with that edition. It's a good idea to keep several catechisms available in class for your learners to use.

Color Key for Teacher Notes

Tan = Specific additional assessments

Blue = Extra activities or questions

Green = Educational tips and directions for specific activities

Gold = Explanations of theological concepts or background for the teacher

Is the Creation Account True?

Timeless Truth

God created the heavens and the earth, He has redeemed His creation, and He will restore it.

Lesson Focus

The learner will be able to explain that God created the universe in six days.

The order, design, and moral order of the creation all point toward a Creator rather than to random chance. Without the Creator, the entire universe hinges on just random chance, which can't possibly explain the complexity of the created world.

14 Is the Creation Account True?

Consider This

Knowing the Truth

As we try to understand the creation of the world, we first need to understand the existence of God. God reveals Himself through His creation and through His Word. Take a brief look at three of the arguments for the existence of God and think of examples that uphold each philosophy.

Cosmology: the study of the world's workings. Everything has a cause.

Teleology: the study of design and purpose. Every design has a designer.

Moral Order: a sense of right and wrong. Every law has a lawgiver.

These are very abstract concepts. Some learners will grasp these better than others. Be sensitive to learners who may get overwhelmed by this discussion.

Think About It . . .

Why is the understanding that God exists necessary to the understanding of creation?

I can explain that God created the universe in six days.

57

God created the heavens and the earth, He has redeemed His creation, and He will restore it.

Unit 4: Beginnings

As the Lord lays out His Law for the Israelites in **Exodus 20**, He reminds them of the fact that He created the universe in six days and then rested on the seventh day. By this, He establishes the Sabbath.

Learners may question the concept of twenty-four-hour days for creation. Critics of twenty-four-hour creation days often point to 2 Peter 3:8: "With the Lord one day is as a thousand years, and a thousand years as one day." However, this reference is talking about the Second Coming of Christ, not creation, so the comparison is incorrect. The days of creation are marked as "evening and morning," the way in which the Hebrew people marked a twenty-four-hour day (sunset to sunset).

Digging Deeper

Six Days to Create

The Book of Genesis outlines a six-day creation account. Individuals with an evolutionary worldview reject the idea of a literal six-day creation, substituting instead millions or even billions of years for the creation of the universe. Since God was the only witness to the creation, we need to look for other clues in order to know the truth.

In the Genesis account of the creation, the Hebrew word for "day" is *yom*, which means a twenty-four-hour period. The other clue is the use of "evening" and "morning," which reflect the Hebrew way of marking time in one twenty-four-hour day.

How does **Exodus 20:9–11** support the six-day creation?

58

Young Earth vs. Old Earth

Your worldview affects your opinion about the age of the earth. Those with a creationist worldview mark the earth's age at approximately six thousand years, while evolutionists say the earth is actually billions of years old.

Why is there such a huge difference between the suggested ages of the earth?

Evolutionists date the earth using radiocarbon dating. What are the potential problems with this method of dating rocks?

What do you think the earth looked like when God created it? How would this affect mankind's modern-day attempts to determine the age of the earth?

False Assumptions

Read or listen to **Question 122** and its answer in your catechism. Outline here the false beliefs concerning creation.

Atheistic Evolution:

Theistic Evolution:

59

Evolutionary theory requires immense amounts of time in order to "work." By contrast, creation took only six twenty-four-hour days.

Radiocarbon dating assumes an old earth and that radioactive materials break down at a constant rate. However, this assumption is unproven, and the margin of error for radiocarbon dating is enormous. Newly formed volcanic rocks date at millions of years because the testing assumes extreme age.

God likely created an earth with age. The trees were not all saplings. Plants were mature enough to provide food. So the earth appeared to have "age" even when newly created.

Atheistic evolution assumes there is no God and no outside interference in the life of the world. The world has no special purpose, and mankind is just like any other creature.

Theistic evolution assumes that the Bible may be God's Word in part but that it cannot be all reliable, since science seems to disprove creation. God may be the Creator, but He used evolutionary methods to accomplish the creation.

These questions aren't meant for learners to work on all by themselves. Either work on them as an entire class or divide into pairs or trios for learners to work through questions together before sharing with the class.

The two consecutive creation summaries in Genesis 1 and 2 do not contradict each other. Rather, Genesis 2 focuses on the creation of humankind as God's unique and special creation.

In his Gospel, John reminds us that Jesus, the Word made flesh, was present at the creation. Our Savior from sin was there before we even came to be by the very hand of God.

The evolutionary model requires death in order for change to occur. But God doesn't include death in that which He calls "very good." Rather, He sends Jesus to save us from sin and death.

You may have some learners who will want to debate all of these ideas and others who will accept them without much discussion. If you have extra time, learners could make posters showing the different theories and why they don't jibe with the biblical truth.

Connections

Jesus, Genesis, and You

Skim **Genesis 1** and **2:4–25**. What is the difference between these creation accounts? Why is this difference important?

In the beginning was the Word, and the Word was with God, and the Word was God. He was in the beginning with God. All things were made through Him, and without Him was not any thing made that was made. John 1:1–3

How does Jesus—the Word made flesh—connect to the creation story?

60

Checks for Understanding

Before your learners leave, consider ways you can give them feedback for next week.

- **Draw It:** Challenge learners to illustrate the days of creation on a series of six note cards or small pieces of paper.
- **Learning Log:** Have learners record in their Learning Log one question they still have about the biblical creation account.

What Do We Know about Evolution?

Timeless Truth

God created the heavens and the earth, He has redeemed His creation, and He will restore it.

Lesson Focus

The learner will share that the world was created by God, not a chance product of evolution.

15 What Do We Know about Evolution?

Consider This

Evolutionary Assumptions

What assumptions does an evolutionary worldview make about . . .

God created the heavens and the earth, He has redeemed His creation, and He will restore it.

Unit 4: Beginnings

I will share that the world was created by God, not a chance product of evolution.

61

Evolution assumes there is no God.

Evolution assumes that the natural realm is all that we have. There can be no supernatural realm.

For the theory of evolution to work, it requires extreme amounts of time. Therefore, evolution assumes an "old earth."

In science, a law is a scientific observation that appears to always be true. A scientific theory is based on observation and repeated trials or observations. Although evolution is labeled a theory, it fails to meet the definition of a theory since it cannot be proven or tested. Most evolution advocates teach this theory as if it were a fact.

Learners who attend public school will have learned scientific theories about the creation of the earth as truth. Or their parents may have taught or reinforced these theories as truth at home. Be sensitive to the struggle this causes for learners. Always keep turning the learner and the discussion to God's Word without criticizing or being negative about the learners' parents or teachers.

Review the faults in the big bang theory and how it doesn't work as a worldview because it does not fit facts.

Guide learners as they suggest their own ideas concerning why the big bang is a big bust.

You may have learners in your group with special needs who might not have covered the theories and concepts on these pages in depth in school yet. Be sensitive not to overwhelm or be condescending to learners who may be on a different academic level than other learners.

Digging Deeper

Big Bang or Big Bust?

The big bang theory states that all the matter in the universe was compressed into a small point until it finally exploded. But is the big bang really just a big bust? Below are some of the problems with the big bang theory. Add one of your own.

62

The Evolution of Life

One more law to know: the law of biogenesis states that life comes only from living things. How does knowing this law help answer these evolutionary claims?

- Chemicals in an early ocean combined to form single-celled organisms.
- Directed panspermia is the claim that the first living cells on earth came from beyond our solar system.

Mutants

In comic books, mutations result in superheroes with special abilities and powers. In the real world, the results of mutations are much different. Yet evolutionists insist that mutations have brought about the kinds of changes that have moved life from single-celled organisms to human life. Three main problems exist with this idea:

1. Mutations never form new types of life. Bacteria forms only bacteria, plants always form new plants.
2. Mutations are almost always harmful, due to the loss of genetic material. Almost all mutations are sterile, unable to reproduce.
3. There are no transitional mutations alive today, nor any transitional fossils as evidence to past mutant organisms.

63

Chemicals forming life directly contradicts the law of biogenesis, since chemicals are nonliving things.

One has to wonder how living cells supposedly made it through the vacuum of space. And consider the irony: evolutionists reject the idea of a divine Creator but will accept the idea of alien life giving rise to life on earth.

Review the concept of mutations and the faults in this concept as a method of evolution.

Help learners understand the difference between the scientific fantasy of macroevolution and the easily observable microevolution. Our Christian faith is not challenged by the scientific reality of microevolution. Examples of microevolution include the many breeds of dogs, cats, and other domestic animals. Learners could also include crops and other plants. Note that many of these microevolutions may be manipulated by humankind.

CONNECTIONS

Evolution's Reality

"But wait a minute," I hear you saying. "What about when bacteria become resistant to antibiotics? Or what about those insects that don't die even after you spray them with bug spray? Doesn't that prove evolution?"

"Well," I would say, "that depends on what kind of evolution you are talking about."

Macroevolution

Organisms change from one kind to another. For example: a fish crawls out of the water and turns into a reptile. Or a chimp decides to stand up one day and become a gorilla, who stands even taller to become a human. Macroevolution is theoretical and unobserved.

Microevolution

Organisms change within their own type. Bacteria become resistant to antibiotics, but they remain bacteria. An insect may change in its reaction to bug killer, but it's still an insect. Microevolution is both observable and scientific.

Think About It . . .

Microevolution is readily observable.

What are some examples of microevolution you can observe in our world today?

64

If you have very concrete learners, there may not be much discussion or question about these theories. Other learners may be quite confused by it all. Prepare by making some visual cues to explain these different types of evolution.

Checks for Understanding

Before your learners leave, consider ways you can give them feedback for next week.

- **Quiz Questions:** Ask learners to write out one quiz question from this lesson. Use their questions to review before the next lesson.
- **Learning Log:** Have learners use their Learning Log to record additional examples of microevolution.

Why Does the Account of Adam and Eve Matter?

Timeless Truth

God created the heavens and the earth, He has redeemed His creation, and He will restore it.

Lesson Focus

The learner will explain that the first chapters of Genesis lay a foundation for fundamental teachings of the faith.

Keep in mind that some of your learners might have similar thoughts. Others may be tempted to be harsh toward the hypothetical persons. Remind the class to speak the truth in love. You may decide to work through each question together, or you may assign pairs to work through one question.

16 Why Does the Account of Adam and Eve Matter?

Consider This

Have you ever heard these statements before? Circle the ones you've heard. If you've heard other similar statements, add those too.

"It doesn't matter whether creation really happened. I believe in God anyway."

"Sure, God made the universe. He just used evolution to do it."

"What's the big deal? Adam and Eve probably didn't exist, but Jesus did."

So what do you think? Does it really matter whether the accounts in Genesis 1–4 actually happened?

Think About It . . .

For those who don't think the first chapters of the Bible are true, at which chapter do they start believing in the truthfulness of the Bible?

I can explain that the first chapters of Genesis lay a foundation for fundamental teachings of the faith.

God created the heavens and the earth, He has redeemed His creation, and He will restore it.

Learners will quickly see that many of the truths of Christianity find their beginnings in Genesis.

First of all, whenever we want to see God's perfect will for work, life, families, and the like, we look to creation before the fall. Because it was perfect, we know it was what God intended.

1. God's Garden of Eden was physical. Creation, people, and animals are all good. God often uses garden themes to describe paradise.

2. We are to take care of God's creation. God told Adam to work before the fall. When sin came, work became hard. But work is a gift from God.

3. God made a man and a woman. They have equal worth with different roles. God told them to be fruitful before sin came into the world, so sex is a good gift of God.

4. The only aspect "not good" in creation, according to God, was that it was not good for man to be alone. Women are an essential part of God's creation.

5. Generations wonder why evil exists. We'll explore this more in a later lesson, but sin entering the world gives sense to the senseless evil in the world.

Digging Deeper

God's Word

Again and again, this course has reinforced the validity of the Bible. If we doubt one piece of the Bible, we don't really have a right to use any of it as an authority. What's worse, if we doubt parts of the Bible, we can easily begin to doubt all of it, which means we doubt God Himself and what He has told us.

Let that sink in: when we don't believe any part of the Bible, we're calling God a liar.

Then, let's look at more specific reasons why an understanding of the first chapters of the Bible shape our understanding of the Bible altogether.

Adam

We might think that we can ignore who Adam is and be fine with the rest of the Bible, but Adam is talked about throughout the Bible. He's mentioned in the New Testament, even as far as Jude, the second-to-last (*penultimate*, if you want to learn a new word) book of the Bible. Adam and his family tree is used to mark spans of time. His name is used when we talk about Baptism. His name is used when we talk about Jesus. That's a lot to dig into at the moment, but if Adam and Eve didn't exist, the message of the Bible changes dramatically.

Foundational Teachings

Let's think about the first few chapters of Genesis. (Go ahead and open your Bible if you don't remember the specifics.)

1. What does the Garden of Eden tell us about paradise?

2. What does paradise tell us about work?

3. What does paradise tell us about marriage?

4. What does paradise tell us about women?

5. What does the first sin tell us about evil?

66

These are very abstract concepts and topics. Your learners will likely be at somewhat different places developmentally. Some learners will be able to easily process this type of information and talk about it with ease; others may be more concrete in their thinking and struggle to make sense of it. This may cause some learners to be less engaged, or it may cause some to behave immaturely. Other learners may be at a more abstract level of thinking, which brings its own set of struggles. Be sensitive to the way learners' cognitive needs play out behaviorally.

6. What does God's response to evil tell us about sin?

7. What does God's response to Adam and Eve's sin tell us about Jesus?

You see, there are so many questions about life that can be answered by understanding how we all got here. Let's try to answer the following questions using what we know about Genesis. Pick two and write your response below.

Do men and women even really need each other?

Is sex a bad thing?

Why do bad things happen?

I keep sinning! Why?

Why did Jesus need to come and die for us?

67

6. God is very clear: sin results in death. Further, God would not want us to live forever in a world tainted by sin. This understanding sets the stage for God's plan of salvation in Jesus. If there was no Adam and Eve, there is no reason for there to be sin in the world. If there is no sin in the world, we do not need Jesus to save us from it. We are all conceived in sin now, and we need a Savior at every age of our life.

7. God's punishments for Adam and Eve explain many hardships. But His love and grace are there as well. He clothes them with animal skins (something had to die to cover their shame). Immediately after the first sin, God gives the first promise of the Savior. Adam and Eve know that their offspring will someday come to rescue them from death.

If you have learners for whom writing is difficult, or some who are uncomfortable or unsure of answering these questions alone, divide them into small groups or pairs to talk together about each question. Or talk about the questions in your large group, being careful to involve only those who feel comfortable.

Connections

The Gospel

If we were to summarize the entire Christian faith in a few bullet points, it might look like this:

- God made everything perfect.
- We sinned, and now there is evil in the world. We deserve to die, and we need a Savior.
- God loves you. He sent His Son to die for you. He rose again and promises life with Him to everyone who believes this.
- Jesus will come again someday. He promises that we will rise again and that He will make a new creation, a new heaven and a new earth. The tree of life and a paradise awaits.

Now, cross out everything that doesn't make sense if Genesis 1–4 is not true.

Make a Plan

If someone asks you if belief in creation and Adam and Eve matter, what would you say? Practice your thoughts below. Maybe think of a specific person and consider Law and Gospel, worldview, and truth in love.

68

Essentially, all of these statements will get crossed out. The Christian truths of forgiveness of sins and complete restoration simply do not make sense without believing the Book of Genesis. To reject the first chapters of the Bible is incompatible with the Christian faith.

For learners who aren't strong readers, read these aloud as you work on them.

Are your learners community-minded? Perhaps they care about environmental or poverty issues. Show how the doctrine of creation supports a Christian approach to both. God tells us to care for His creation, and He promises to restore all creation someday. We can be caretakers of creation now and await the new heavens and earth when Christ returns. Similarly, when we care for our neighbor, we point to the restoration of all things in Christ. This can be exciting for those who wrestle with messages about evolution and environment and the like. Invite learners to make posters that promote awareness of these issues with a Christian perspective.

Checks for Understanding

Before your learners leave, consider ways you can give them feedback for next week.

- **Strength in Numbers:** Turn "Make a Plan" into a group event. Invite learners to offer up scenarios that they've encountered. Invite the class to support one another with ideas. This reinforces the idea that we support one another in defending the faith. It also gives you an opportunity to reinforce tactics and strategies that are helpful.
- **Take It Home:** Ask learners to write down one question they still have. Tell them to share this question with their family and to write a response and return it next week.

Is There Evidence of the Flood?

Timeless Truth

God created the heavens and the earth, He has redeemed His creation, and He will restore it.

Lesson Focus

The learner will understand that through a worldwide flood God cleansed the earth and saved Noah and his family.

17 IS THERE EVIDENCE OF THE FLOOD?

CONSIDER THIS

A UNIVERSAL FLOOD

Moses records the account of Noah, his family, and the universal flood in Genesis 6–9.

> The LORD saw that the wickedness of man was great in the earth, and that every intention of the thoughts of his heart was only evil continually.
> Genesis 6:5

> Noah was a righteous man, blameless in his generation. Noah walked with God.
> Genesis 6:9

THINK ABOUT IT . . .

How can you explain the contrast between these two verses from Genesis 6?

Did You Know?

- There are more than 270 historical accounts of worldwide floods outside of the Bible.
- The Hawaiian flood account tells of a man named Nu-u and his family, who build a canoe with a house on it and filled it with animals.
- One Chinese flood account says the man took his three sons and three daughters aboard a boat to survive a flood that covered the highest mountains. Paintings of this account depict a dove with an olive branch flying toward the boat.
- The Toletecs in Mexico tell of a flood that came 1,716 years after the creation (this fits the biblical genealogy). After the flood, the people started building a tall tower to protect themselves from the next flood, but their languages became confused so they had to abandon the project.

GOD CREATED THE HEAVENS AND THE EARTH, HE HAS REDEEMED HIS CREATION, AND HE WILL RESTORE IT.

UNIT 4: BEGINNINGS

I can tell how, through a worldwide flood, God cleansed the earth and saved Noah and his family.

69

Reading all of Genesis 6–9 will likely take too much time. Start by finding out what learners already know about the flood account. Then, go to Scripture and have learners skim to find whether their assumptions and knowledge are correct. Depending on the makeup of your class, you could do this in small groups.

The contrast between these two quotes just a few verses apart in Genesis 6 demonstrates the difference in the world at that time. The world had become incredibly evil, yet in the midst of all this evil, Noah and his family remained faithful to God.

If the worldwide flood account in Genesis is made up, how could such diverse cultures contain stories that are so similar to the biblical account?

Help learners identify what pieces of this Scripture account are commonly misunderstood or even portrayed incorrectly in popular culture's telling of this story.

Do this by reading aloud sections of print rather than relying only on learners to read to themselves.

Since the Bible is God's Word, we can trust in its entire reliability. Knowing that the flood account contains verifiable information reassures believers about the truth of the entire Bible.

Digging Deeper

An Ark Encounter

Outside of Williamstown, Kentucky, crowds board a bus and head into the wooded countryside. As they come over the hill, they suddenly see a gigantic wooden ship on the horizon. Built according to biblical specifications, the Ark Encounter invites visitors to experience the history and science behind the flood account found in Genesis 6–9. Take a look at some of the information visitors can find at the Ark Encounter.

Ethnic Diversity?

If Noah and his family had medium-colored skin, they could have easily given rise to all skin colors on earth today.

Will It Float?

Marine engineers say the design and dimensions of the ark match those of modern ocean-going commercial ships.

Room for the Animals?

The dimension of the ark provided over 1.5 million cubic feet of interior space. Scientists estimate there were probably about 16,000 individual animals on the ark. This would only have taken about half of the space available.

Water Everywhere?

If the earth were smooth like a billiard ball, there would be more than enough surface water to cover the entire globe 1.9 miles deep. The biblical description of the "fountains of the great deep burst[ing] forth" explains some of the massive changes that occurred on the earth in the flood.

Think About It . . .

How does it help knowing that the biblical flood account is accurate?

70

Rock-Solid Evidence

A worldwide flood would certainly leave behind evidence in the geological record. As you study the account of the flood, consider this evidence:

Folded Sediment: The Grand Canyon and other locations around the world show folded layers of sedimentary rock. This is not possible unless the rocks experienced great upheaval from earthquakes or shifts in the earth's crust.

Aquatic Fossils: Fossilized shark teeth are regularly found in Wyoming. Shells and other aquatic fossils appear on the Himalaya Mountains in Nepal.

Fossil Beds: Massive fossil graveyards, with mixtures of animal species, exist in North America, Siberia, and other places around the world. Massive coal beds, made from compressed plants and animals, are found around the world.

Mount St. Helens: The massive volcanic eruption in 1980 changed the rules about sedimentary deposits. In the minutes following the eruption, layers were deposited in a way that was previously thought to have taken millions of years.

Climate Change: Recent Antarctic expeditions have discovered fossilized remains of a thick forest that once covered much of the continent, indicating that the climate was once very different there from its present frozen condition.

Fault Lines/Plate Tectonics: When the "fountains of the great deep burst forth" (Genesis 7:11), the earth's crust fractured and bent, causing mountain ranges to rise up while other areas sank, forming the ocean depths.

71

Review the geologic evidence for the flood. If time allows, have learners search online for images related to each of these topics.

Read aloud sections of print rather than relying only on learners reading to themselves.

Some learners may have additional questions about dinosaurs and the geologic evidence. The majority of dinosaurs were not the giant T. Rex, Triceratops, and Allosaurus we see displayed in museums. Most were no larger than dogs. Unlike most animal species, reptiles like dinosaurs continue to grow throughout their lifetime. In other words, very large dinosaurs were very old dinosaurs.

Most dinosaur skeletons on display in museums are assembled from much smaller bone fragments, since the fossils excavated are far from complete. The completed skeletons and models are based on the "best guess" of scientists. The well-known T. Rex skeleton of Sue, located at the Field Museum in Chicago, was recently cleaned and reconfigured because museum scientists realized that they had incorrectly positioned the skeleton when it was first displayed.

Luther's flood prayer tells how God used the flood to cleanse the world's sin. In the same way, God uses the waters of Baptism to cleanse us of our sin.

Water was present from the very creation of our earth, and God used water again to recreate through the flood. But God also promised to never again flood the whole earth.

Option: Talk about how the church is like an ark.

Option: Use the "Think about It" questions as starting points for group discussion, or have learners use them for a "think-pair-share" activity.

CONNECTIONS

ARK IMPLICATIONS

In the liturgy for Holy Baptism, you find a "flood prayer" written by Martin Luther. The prayer opens with these lines:

> *"Almighty and eternal God, according to Your strict judgment You condemned the unbelieving world through the flood, yet according to Your great mercy You preserved believing Noah and his family, eight souls in all. . . ."*

THINK ABOUT IT . . .

How does the prayer connect the flood account to Holy Baptism?

> **For they deliberately overlook this fact, that the heavens existed long ago, and the earth was formed out of water and through water by the word of God, and that by means of these the world that then existed was deluged with water and perished. But by the same word the heavens and earth that now exist are stored up for fire, being kept until the day of judgment and destruction of the ungodly.**
>
> **2 Peter 3:5–7**

THINK ABOUT IT . . .

What is the role of water in both the creation and the re-creation of the earth?

72

CHECKS FOR UNDERSTANDING

Before your learners leave, consider ways you can give them feedback for next week.

- **Float Your Boat:** Have learners use a variety of craft materials to create their own arks. If time allows, see whose ark has the greatest capacity: float the boats in a small tub of water, and load each ark with small plastic animals. The winner is the ark that can hold the most animals without sinking.
- **Learning Log:** Learners can use their Learning Log to record one new fact they learned about the flood account in today's lesson.

Is the God of the Old Testament the Same God of the New Testament?

Timeless Truth

God created the heavens and the earth, He has redeemed His creation, and He will restore it.

Lesson Focus

The learner will be able to explain that God is the same yesterday, today, and forever.

18 Is the God of the Old Testament the Same God of the New Testament?

Consider This

Have you ever heard these statements before? Circle the ones you've heard. If you've heard other similar statements, add those too.

"The Old Testament God is mean and angry all the time. I like Jesus better."

"Well, that rule doesn't really matter anymore. It was written in the Old Testament."

"The Jewish people have their God from the Old Testament. We have Jesus."

Think About It . . .

If the Old Testament God and the New Testament God are different, when did they switch? Or when did God decide to stop being Himself?

I am able to explain that God is the same yesterday, today, and forever.

73

Unit 4: Beginnings

God created the heavens and the earth, He has redeemed His creation, and He will restore it.

The third statement is an especially dangerous belief held by many Christians. In Genesis, God promised the Savior for all nations. If Jesus is the way, the truth, and the life, we cannot ignore our Jewish neighbors when we share the Gospel.

Some religions claim to worship the God of Abraham and even regard the Old Testament writings as sacred, but they reject the triune God by rejecting His salvation in Jesus Christ. See **John 5:19–23, 39–47**.

This activity may be tough! And that's okay. This far into the course, it's good to try to prompt learners to think of their own examples from the Bible as practice for real life. If learners can think of key words, show them how a concordance or online Bible search tool can help them find what they need.

If learners are younger or if they get stuck, you can provide them with examples.

Isaiah 52, **Psalm 22**, and hundreds of other Old Testament prophecies point to Jesus.

The Books of Matthew and Hebrews are very intentional in using the Old Testament to point out where Jesus fulfills those prophecies.

If talking through their answers is more helpful, have learners do that before trying to write a response.

Digging Deeper

Scripture Study

The great news about this topic is that the person who is talking about an Old and New Testament God already knows that there is an Old Testament, a New Testament, and God. The best approach to talk about the Old Testament and New Testament would, of course, be to use the Old Testament and the New Testament. Let's dig into the Bible!

Cross Connections

Can you think of passages in the Old Testament that point to Jesus? You don't have to give specific references, just give a brief description or key words.

Can you think of passages in the New Testament that point to the Old Testament? Again, you can just describe the section or maybe think of some key words.

74

Eternal God

Let's see what God has to say about Himself. Choose a few references, and write down key words or the main point in your own words.

John 1:1–5

John 10:30

Revelation 21:6

Hebrews 13:8

John 5:37–39

Matthew 5:17

Job 38:4–7

Matthew 1:22–23

Numbers 23:19

Psalm 90:2

Law and Gospel

Sometimes, people think of the Old Testament as being the Law and the New Testament as being the Gospel. Throughout the entire Bible, our triune God gives both. Let's find some examples of the Gospel in the Old Testament and some Law in the New Testament.

Old Testament	New Testament
Genesis 26:4	Matthew 5:48
Isaiah 9:6	Matthew 18:16
Isaiah 43:1	Mark 11:15–18
Jeremiah 31:3	Luke 17:2

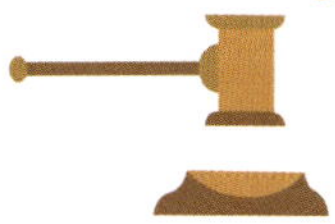

75

This activity intentionally shows a long list of examples, but it may be too difficult or involved for your learners to go through the entire list. You can assign certain passages to small groups, divide the list by writing the references on slips of paper and drawing them out of a bowl, or work through them together, ending after a designated amount of time. You could send some passages home so that learners can look over them with their caregivers.

This is also a good opportunity for learners to practice using their Bible app to listen to Scripture.

Again, you may want to assign passages to small groups for this activity.

The point behind the argument here is that often people want to dismiss a command of God as outdated. For example, they may try to equate God's laws about homosexuality with those for eating certain meats. A careful study of Scripture shows that this reasoning does not hold up.

If it comes up, note that the discussion on divorce can be a difficult one, but it can also provide a fruitful discussion about God's intent for marriage: two virgins of the opposite gender marrying each other and remaining faithful until death. God does not single out homosexuality, sex outside of marriage, or divorce.

Take care to demonstrate God's truth in love, and use a balance of Law and Gospel as an example to the group as you answer questions that may arise.

Also keep in mind that gender identity will be discussed in a later lesson.

Help learners with reading struggles to locate these Scripture passages in their Bibles by marking them prior to class, printing them on note cards, or teaching them to use a Bible app. Let them use that same app to listen to these passages.

CONNECTIONS

DOES THIS STILL APPLY?

The Bible is clear: God is God from everlasting to everlasting, and He does not change. In the Old Testament, God showed the seriousness of sin and the need for the promised Savior. In the New Testament, the promised Savior died a horrific death because of the seriousness of sin. Both Old and New Testament have Law and Gospel. Both have difficult truths and beautiful blessings. In the Old Testament, the Savior was prophesied and foreshadowed. In the New Testament, the Savior fulfilled those prophecies.

One of the reasons why people want to separate the Old and New Testaments is because of the rules. They want to believe that all the rules of the Old Testament don't really matter. But that's because they don't take a close look at those Old Testament rules.

In the Old Testament, God's people followed some laws about worship. Those laws reminded them that they were set apart from the world and that sacrifice was needed for sin. Those laws pointed to Jesus.

There were also governmental laws, much like we have today for our government. Some of those laws don't apply anymore because we do not have the same government.

There was also God's moral law, such as the Ten Commandments. Those do not change. We have those today.

How can we tell the difference? The New Testament is very clear on this. For instance, the New Testament clearly says that the ceremonial laws about what foods to eat don't apply anymore (see **Acts 10:9–15**). In other words, God wrote down which rules were canceled. The New Testament also reaffirms many laws. Take a look at some of the laws that the New Testament underscores:

Matthew 19:3–9

Mark 7:21–23

1 Corinthians 6:9–10

Galatians 5:18–21

SUM IT UP

There is a lot to sort through here! Write down two new things you learned today.

1.

2.

76

CHECKS FOR UNDERSTANDING

Before your learners leave, consider ways you can give them feedback for next week.

- **Sum It Up:** This lesson covers a great deal of material. Walk around the room as learners write down two new things they learned to discern what caught their attention today and perhaps what might need further discussion later.
- **Top Questions:** Place a box in the room and invite learners to each write one question on a piece of paper and deposit it in the box. Within that week, send out a group email to all learners and parents to answer the questions. If you need to limit it, tell them that you will address the five most common questions of the group.

UNIT 5: CHRISTIAN LIFE

TIMELESS TRUTH

God has called me to be His own and uses me to witness the truth in love with my neighbor.

ESSENTIAL QUESTION

What is God's will for me as I live the Christian life?

FOCUS STATEMENTS

19. The learner will be able to share that in Christ, he or she is a loved and forgiven child of God.
20. The learner will be able to explain that life begins at conception and that all life matters to God.
21. The learner will share how he or she can be a faithful Christian and still love science.
22. The learner will witness to the fact that although we live in a fallen world because of sin, God will restore all things through the victory He gives in Christ.
23. The learner will share that there are nonphysical creatures: angels who serve God and demons who try to lead us away from God.
24. The learner will be able to explain that ghosts and aliens are deceptions created to distract from the true God.
25. The learner will witness to the facts that hell is a place created for the devil and his demons, and that Jesus rescues us from hell, which we deserve, and welcomes us to be with Him in heaven, which will be made new.
26. The learner will share examples of how God uses ordinary means to aid us in times of need now and in the future.
27. The learner will be able to tell that he or she is redeemed and free to love God and others, and equipped by God to serve his or her neighbor and tell others about Jesus.
28. The learner will describe that God is the creator and authority for marriage, which is a picture of Christ and His Church.
29. The learner will share with others that God has created him or her uniquely male or female.
30. The learner will express that God is with us and gives us what we need to defend the faith and witness to those who need to hear of their Savior.

ASSESSMENT OPTIONS

1. **Preassessment Options**

   Before you begin this unit, have each learner spend a few minutes writing down or telling you a partner their answers to the following.

   - Who am I?
   - Who gets the final say in issues that have to do with life, morality, and the like?
   - How can I defend the faith?

   After they have written these down, either collect the answers (to read and leave feedback) or quickly go over them together as a class. You'll get a sense of where each learner is coming from as you begin.
2. **Formative Assessment Options**
   a. Learning Log: After each class, have learners write in their Learning Log one important thing they discovered in that class.
   b. Reflection Tools: Learners will likely be in the practice of using reflection tools now. Remind them that these can be of help in the future when they will want to return to their notes as resources in everyday life.
3. **Summative Assessment Options**
   a. Learning Portfolio: Have learners complete a variety of formative assessments over the course of this unit. At the end of the unit, they will compile at least one of each type of formative assessment, along with completed

lesson notes and other samples you require. Learners who complete these tasks over the course of the unit will find them to be a great summative assessment. This unit is the last, so you may choose to collect the entire portfolio during this time. You may want to set aside a time when learners pick one or two pieces from their portfolio to present to the class. *Note*: At the beginning of the unit, make a list of samples you will collect so there are no surprises at the end.

b. Class Presentation: Schedule a time to invite family and friends! Organize learners in groups or ask them to work together as a class to articulate their faith regarding their learning in this unit. Not only will this presentation serve as a witness to others, but it will also be evidence of what has been learned throughout the course.

   You may write your own questions to guide the presentation or use the following questions based on the unit:

   - What is my identity?
   - What do I need to know about the world I cannot see (angels, heaven, etc.)?
   - What do I need to know as I defend the faith?

Teaching Tips

1. This unit may be highly anticipated by your learners as it takes on some frequently asked questions. Learners will likely differ in which lessons they are most interested based on their own curiosity and what they have been asked by friends. Remind learners that especially for these issues, worldview is important. Christians can and do use the Bible as a chief source of authority. Others do not. Sometimes, Christians need to take a step back and establish some foundational truths about God and the Bible before digging into the more provocative topics. After all, that reality informed the scope and sequence of this course. Perhaps more than any other unit, this one might exhibit a wide array of beliefs. Your learners are trying to embrace both the Bible and society's views on identity and the like, so patiently reminder them of the basic truths you've already covered throughout the course and show how these truths impact the issues in question. Again, exhibit patience, respect, and truth in love to provide an example for your learners.
2. Remember that participants will vary in learning from topic to topic. Throughout the previous units, you've seen how some of your learners are more familiar with the catechism than others. You may have already seen that at times you need to work through more foundational knowledge. Other times, a lesson might revisit something learners know well but may still challenge them, as the lessons in this course come from an angle of articulating the faith to others. That said, there will be times when the learners themselves will need some convincing. In other words, it's critical that you use your discretion to pick and choose the parts of the lessons you want to spend the most time on, based on your learners' prior knowledge. Remember, you are aiming for learning. Always ask yourself: Do my learners better understand the content of the Timeless Truth and the Lesson Focus? How do I know? Keep returning to this.
3. Again, this entire curriculum uses the 2017 edition of *Luther's Small Catechism with Explanation*. The references to the Questions will match only with that edition. It's a good idea to keep a catechism or two available for your learners to use when needed.

Color Key for Teacher Notes

Tan = Specific additional assessments

Blue = Extra activities or questions

Green = Educational tips and directions for specific activities

Gold = Explanations of theological concepts or background for the teacher

What Is My Identity?

Timeless Truth

God has called me to be His own and uses me to witness the truth in love with my neighbor.

Lesson Focus

The learner will be able to share that in Christ, he or she is a loved and forgiven child of God.

This unit kicks off many questions that have to do with the Christian life and Christian worldview. Most times, these questions are primarily answered with the Bible as the authority. This is why the previous lessons that established Jesus as trustworthy, God as real, and God's Word as true were so important. Occasionally, you may need to remind learners that some questions are not easy to address with non-Christians because they do not start in the same place as we do. In those cases, backing up and starting with a witness to Jesus as Savior is a better place to begin.

19 What Is My Identity?

Consider This

You have sixty seconds to answer this question: Who are you?

Time's up! Now, consider another question:
Who or what gets to decide who you are?

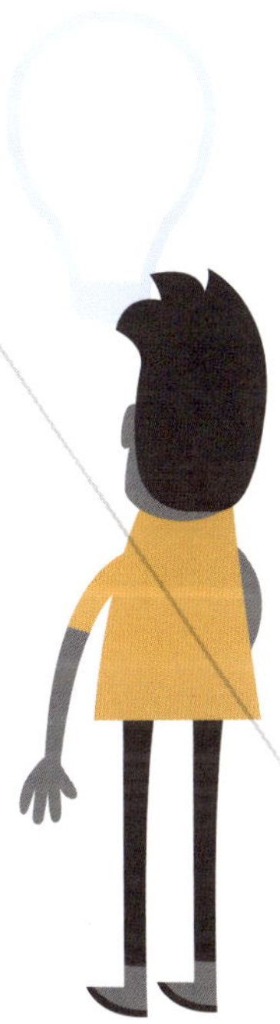

God has called me to be His own and uses me to witness the truth in love with my neighbor.

The Image of God

Genesis 1:26–27 tells us that humans were created in the image of God. What does that mean? It was much more than a physical resemblance. Humans reflected the character of God and represented God in the world. When Adam and Eve sinned, they lost this image of God.

Think About It . . .

How does God restore in us what Adam and Eve had lost?

I am able to share that in Christ, I am a loved and forgiven child of God.

77

Unit 5: Christian Life

These questions are typical parts of adolescent development, but they mean even more today as society tries to grapple with identity issues. Don't avoid the questions, but keep in mind that not everyone will want to answer. Consider sharing first or asking a confident learner to begin, which can help to diffuse tension.

Option: Learners might be more comfortable working through these questions in pairs or small groups, and then presenting to the whole class.

Guide learners to discuss these vignettes either in small groups or in your whole group together. Be sensitive to learners who might be grappling with these exact issues, always sharing the love of Jesus with them first and foremost.

For learners who aren't strong readers, pair them with someone who is comfortable reading the text to their partner. Or you can read the vignettes aloud.

This page hits home at some central assumptions about identity. Who gets to say who you are? On one hand, you probably know yourself better than others do. On the other hand, we are all sinful and sometimes get our identity wrong. Our feelings can get in the way of reality. God is perfect and will always know who we are: His.

Can people decide their gender? What about other physical attributes, such as age, ethnicity, or height? There are some helpful videos online in which Christians explore this question. Search and preview a good illustration of identity.

Digging Deeper

Who Are You?

Let's review the first two questions of this lesson. Who are you? Who or what gets to decide who you are? Because of sin, our identity can get confusing. Sometimes, we don't even know who we are! Think through the following situations.

Rosa is a ballerina, and she is the top dancer in her company. But lately, she doesn't feel very good at all. She watches videos of herself and wonders if she was ever good at ballet. On top of that, she can't believe how she looks. Her friends keep telling her how skinny she is, but when she looks in the mirror, she only sees fat.

Is Rosa right about who she is?

Jake has always worked hard at school, but his math teacher right now doesn't seem to like him. When he makes mistakes, the teacher acts like it's no surprise. When he does well, his teacher looks at him with suspicion, as if he cheated. Jake's never felt more unsure as to who he is as a student. He thought he was a good kid, but maybe his teacher sees something in him that he didn't know before.

Is Jake's teacher right about who he is?

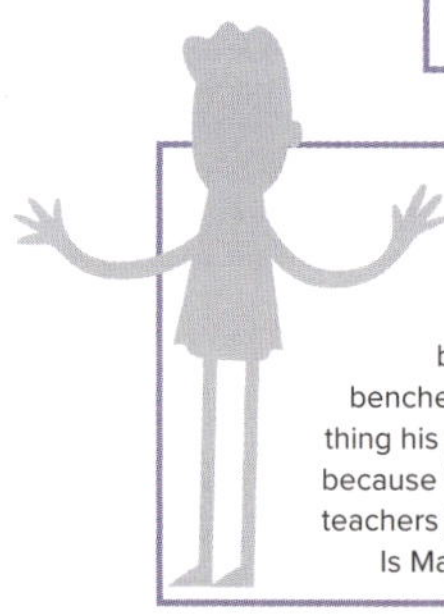

Marcus is the best. Just ask him. He's the smartest kid in class, even if he decides not to turn in his homework all the time. He's really great at basketball, and it makes no sense that he's benched half of the time during games. It's a good thing his parents believe how good of a kid he is, because his constant detentions are caused by his teachers just not understanding him.

Is Marcus right about his identity?

You Know Me Better Than I Do

Take a look at this heading. Have you ever said this to anyone else? Usually, we think we know ourselves better than others do. But sometimes, others see something in us that we never quite knew before.

The one who knows us best is the one who created us. Check it out:

Psalm 139:13 **Isaiah 43:1** **1 Corinthians 6:19–20**

78

You Are Known

God created us, redeemed us, and loves us. He will restore us and raise us up on the Last Day to be with Him. In short, He knows you better than anyone else does. Every person—including you—is tainted by sin. So while we might sometimes get it right, we often get our identity wrong. We can't trust our feelings when our feelings tell us that we are worthless or unloved. We can't trust others when they decide to label us according to their understanding of the world. But in all things, as we've discussed in the past, we can always trust God. So what does God say about us? Read or listen to each passage; then, summarize it.

Luke 8:21

Romans 6:1–11

1 Peter 2:9–10

You Are His

God knows you, He loves you, and He has claimed you as His child in Baptism. Nothing can separate you from His love.

In Baptism, He makes you new. He calls you holy. He restores His image in you. Now, in this world, you live as both a sinner and a saint. But your identity is in Christ, who died and rose for you. Someday, when Jesus returns, you will be wholly holy and completely new. (That's a lot to take in. If this sounds new to you, read over the sections about Baptism in the Small Catechism.)

How does this identity impact the way you consider yourself?

79

Our identity in Christ is essential when we consider who we are, and it is foundational when we consider our calling. If your learners have already gone through the catechism study, this section will be more of a review. If not, you might need to slow down and talk about Baptism for most of the lesson today, using the Small Catechism.

This section is incredibly important when distinguishing God's will and design for us. Some learners will be tempted to say that their temptations are fine because God loves us as we are. Gently remind them that God's Law still applies to them and to all of us. Others will be burdened with self-loathing and need to hear about God's love in the Gospel. Distinguish sinful temptations from physical abilities and the like to help make the difference.

Connections

Sinner Saints

God has given you an identity in Him. Sometimes, we don't like what we see in the mirror, and there are two main reasons for that.

Saint Seeing a Sinner

Sometimes, you look in the mirror, and you realize that you are a sinner. Yes, there are still sins that entangle you. But that sin does not define you. Confess it to God, who forgives you and enables you to fight against temptation for another day. Don't fall into the trap of thinking, "Well, if I want to commit this sin, that must define me as a person." The devil wants you to think that your sin is who you are. You belong to God, and He will help you through the trials you face.

Sinner Not Seeing the Saint

There are other things about us that we don't like: our abilities (or lack thereof), our looks, our gifts, our place in life. This stems from discontent. We don't like who God made us to be. When you start to think this way, ask yourself this question: "This thing I don't like, is it a sin?" If it is a sin, look to the paragraph above. Ask for forgiveness and live as a redeemed child of God. If it is not a sin, then you might actually be sinning in your discontent. Or you're just too beaten down to see the wonderful person God has made you to be. Pray to God about this and read His Word. Check out the Bible passages on the previous page and remember that you are dearly loved with callings that God has given you where you are right now.

Make a Plan

In this lesson, we focused on you and your identity more than usual. When defending the faith, it's important for you to be very sure of your own identity in Christ. And now, you can take the same approaches as you think of ways to talk with others about their identity. Look at the three situations below. Choose one, and practice a response.

Niko loves golf and plays it every week. He's on the golf team at school, but he recently broke his arm. He won't be able to play golf for months. He's not playing golf, so he's not a golfer, right? Then, who is he?

Greg is struggling with a temptation, and it's driving him crazy. He keeps praying about it, but that temptation keeps coming back. He wonders if this is just who he is and figures that it's just a matter of time until he gives in.

Maria can't stand the way she looks. She knows she's ugly. Her hair, her nose, her weight . . . and no one likes her. She doesn't like herself either. She can't help but think she's worthless and unworthy of love.

80

Remind learners that they are children of God and that all their gifts have been given to them by God to be used in His kingdom.

Checks for Understanding

Before your learners leave, consider ways you can give them feedback for next week.

- **Learning Log:** Have learners consider the question, "Who does God say that I am?"
- **Exit Ticket:** Ask learners to hand you their response to "Make a Plan." They probably needed an extra sheet of paper this time around.

Does Human Life Matter? When Does It Begin? When Does It End?

Timeless Truth

God has called me to be His own and uses me to witness the truth in love with my neighbor.

Lesson Focus

The learner will be able to explain that life begins at conception and that all life matters to God.

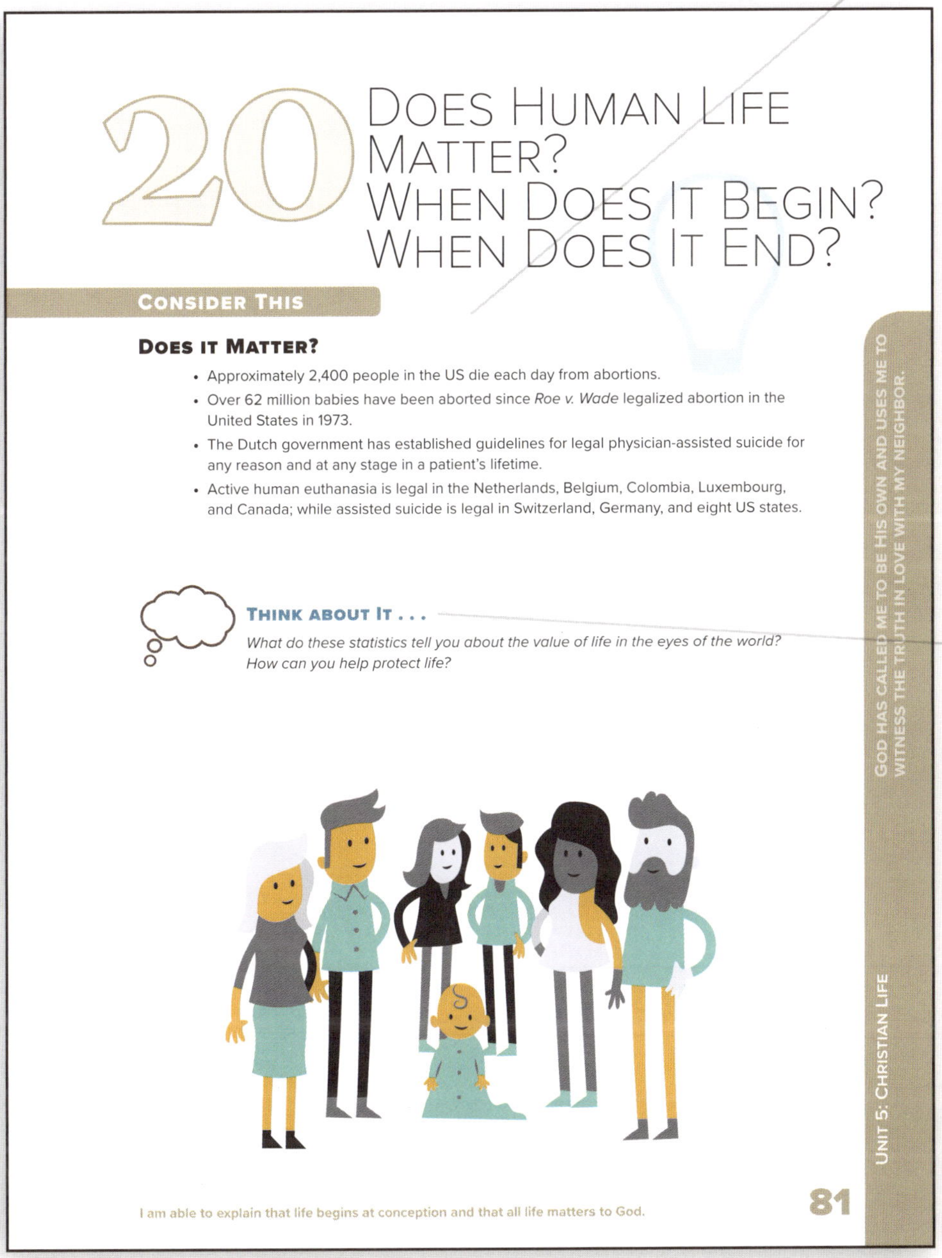

20 Does Human Life Matter? When Does It Begin? When Does It End?

Consider This

Does it Matter?

- Approximately 2,400 people in the US die each day from abortions.
- Over 62 million babies have been aborted since *Roe v. Wade* legalized abortion in the United States in 1973.
- The Dutch government has established guidelines for legal physician-assisted suicide for any reason and at any stage in a patient's lifetime.
- Active human euthanasia is legal in the Netherlands, Belgium, Colombia, Luxembourg, and Canada; while assisted suicide is legal in Switzerland, Germany, and eight US states.

Think About It . . .

What do these statistics tell you about the value of life in the eyes of the world? How can you help protect life?

God has called me to be His own and uses me to witness the truth in love with my neighbor.

Unit 5: Christian Life

I am able to explain that life begins at conception and that all life matters to God.

81

Option: Find a real-life story of someone whose parent chose not to abort him or her even though it seemed like abortion was a good idea. There are many Christian women who are advocates for the unborn who tell their own stories online. Or find a real-life story of a woman whose doctor advised her to abort her unborn baby but she chose not to. Do some research and discussion of these real-life stories before sharing them.

The world shows little value for the life of the unborn, elderly, or ill. As Christians, we can speak out against these practices as we defend those who cannot defend themselves.

In His Word, God shows us the value of every life, even those who are not yet born. He knows our purpose even before we are born. Human life begins at the very moment of conception.

DIGGING DEEPER

BEFORE YOU WERE FORMED

In the Fifth Commandment, God tells us, "You shall not murder." While it would be tempting to say you have never broken this commandment, it's important to understand the full scope of the commandment. Read **Question 62A** and its answer in your catechism; also read the verses below.

What do these verses tell us about the value of an unborn life in the eyes of God? When does life begin in the eyes of God?

Before I formed you in the womb I knew you, and before you were born I consecrated you; I appointed you a prophet to the nations.
Jeremiah 1:5

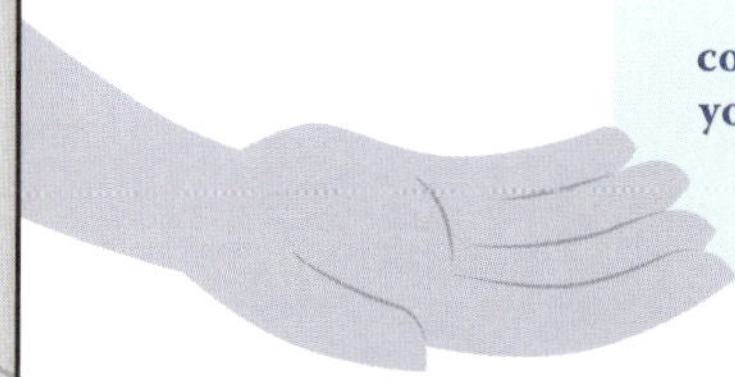

Ask learners to discuss this question: How does it make you feel to know that God knew you and formed you in the womb, even before you mother knew you?

Your eyes saw my unformed substance; in Your book were written, every one of them, the days that were formed for me, when as yet there was none of them.
Psalm 139:16

And when Elizabeth heard the greeting of Mary, the baby leaped in her womb. And Elizabeth was filled with the Holy Spirit, and she exclaimed with a loud cry, "Blessed are you among women, and blessed is the fruit of your womb! And why is this granted to me that the mother of my Lord should come to me? For behold, when the sound of your greeting came to my ears, the baby in my womb leaped for joy."
Luke 1:41–44

82

Roe v. Wade

Some learners may be aware of the Supreme Court decision that legalized abortion in the United States on January 22, 1973. Each January, life-advocacy groups gather in Washington, DC, for the March for Life, a peaceful gathering to support the rights of the unborn. As time allows, discuss with learners how they could help support the cause of life in your congregation and community.

At Life's End

Question 62B in the catechism talks about issues related to the end of life. Read through this section of the catechism and respond to the scenarios below.

But I trust in You, O Lord; I say,
"You are my God."
My times are in Your hand.
Psalm 31:14–15

A. A Christian with a terminal illness chooses to stop fighting the disease and enter hospice care.

B. A person diagnosed with a serious illness that will soon lead to paralysis chooses to seek medication that will result in death.

C. A person is diagnosed with a rapidly growing brain tumor. Chemotherapy is not an option, and surgery might only extend life by a few months. The person chooses not to have the surgery.

D. A person is afraid of losing his mental abilities, so he chooses to end his life.

83

A. Christians can comfortably use hospice services for loved ones or themselves near the end of life. Hospice does nothing to shorten life, but merely works to reduce pain, allowing people to live out their final days in comfort.

B. Seeking to end one's life prematurely goes against God's Word.

C. When a terminal diagnosis is certain, the person certainly has the option not to seek treatment.

D. Taking one's own life is forbidden by God.

Know your learners and plan for the best way to dig into this sensitive material together. One option is to divide your group into pairs or trios to discuss these questions and then share their group's insights with the larger group.

Be sensitive to learners who may have had to deal with these sorts of issues in their families. Point grieving people to God's love and forgiveness in Christ.

Encourage your learners as they work through these very real issues. The catechism provides suggestions and practical advice for dealing with issues related to unplanned pregnancies and those who have experienced an abortion and now deal with the guilt and pain.

While the catechism doesn't address hospice care directly, it does address the difference between allowing death to occur and causing the death of an individual. Hospice care falls into the "allowing death" category. Those in hospice care benefit from visits with friends and family and time spent in prayer and study of God's promises found in His Word.

CONNECTIONS

CARING FOR THE BROKEN

Every day, thousands of women face the challenges of unplanned pregnancy. Our world suggests what it considers an "easy" solution, but one that comes with serious long-term impacts. Review **Question 63** in your Small Catechism and then discuss these situations with one of your classmates.

- Your best friend just found out that she is pregnant. She's frightened to tell her parents and doesn't know quite what to do. How can you help and support her with this challenge?
- You've noticed that your cousin seems to be really struggling with some personal issue. When you talk with her, she confesses that she had an abortion about two months ago. Now she is feeling guilty and depressed and doesn't know what to do. How can you help bring a message of forgiveness and grace to your cousin?
- An elderly aunt has been struggling with a variety of illnesses as she grows older. Recently, she discovered that her pancreatic cancer has spread to other parts of her body. Rather than continuing treatment for her cancer, your aunt has chosen to enter hospice treatment. How can you help and support your aunt at this point in her life?

Lutherans For Life (www.lutheransforlife.org) provides a number of items for the study of life issues. **Lutherans For Life** produces resources for all ages, for training, and for conferences to help Christians deal with abortion, euthanasia, and other life challenges.

84

The illustration here is a perfect reminder for learners that in the midst of all of these very real struggles, God keeps His people close in His hands. Ask learners for their reaction to this illustration.

CHECKS FOR UNDERSTANDING

Before your learners leave, consider ways you can give them feedback for next week.

- **Learning Log:** In their Learning Log, learners can write a thank-you note to their parents for giving them life.
- **Service Project:** Help learners coordinate a congregational gathering of diapers, blankets, and similar items to support a local crisis nursery or other support organization for young mothers.

As a Christian, Can I Like Science?

Timeless Truth

God has called me to be His own and uses me to witness the truth in love with my neighbor.

Lesson Focus

The learner will share how he or she can be a faithful Christian and still love science.

21 As a Christian, Can I Like Science?

Consider This

What are some of the areas of disagreement people see between science and religion?

What can Christians and scientists agree upon?

God has called me to be His own and uses me to witness the truth in love with my neighbor.

Unit 5: Christian Life

I will share how I can be a faithful Christian and still love science.

85

In general, most people consider science and religion as directly opposed to each other in all areas. But the primary disagreement is the origin of the world. See Lessons 14 and 15 for more information.

Some scientists see beyond the hard-and-fast scientific facts. They understand that creation speaks to an orderly creation and therefore some kind of intelligent creator.

Option: Ask learners what they struggle with in regard to their own faith and science.

Have learners match the scientist to the description of their scientific work.

1. D. Pascal
2. E. Newton
3. A. Copernicus
4. C. Galilei
5. F. Herschel
6. B. Bacon
7. L. Einstein
8. J. Planck
9. H. Mendel
10. I. Kelvin
11. G. Faraday
12. K. Curie

If time allows, let learners do some online research to find these answers. Learners can work in pairs or trios to discover the answers.

Digging Deeper

Scientists and God

While not necessarily Christians, these scientists all believed in the concept of a creator God who gave structure and organization to the world. Use online resources to match the scientists to the description of their area of scientific study.

Scientist

A. Nicholas Copernicus (1473–1543)

B. Sir Francis Bacon (1561–1627)

C. Galileo Galilei (1564–1642)

D. Blaise Pascal (1623–1662)

E. Isaac Newton (1642–1727)

F. Caroline Herschel (1750–1848)

G. Michael Faraday (1791–1867)

H. Gregor Mendel (1822–1884)

I. William Kelvin (1824–1907)

J. Max Planck (1858–1947)

K. Marie Curie (1867–1934)

L. Albert Einstein (1879–1955)

Area of Study

___ 1. French mathematician, physicist, inventor, and theologian who established the foundation for probability theory.

___ 2. Best known for his work with defining gravity, this scientist saw God's hand in the structure of mathematics.

___ 3. Polish scientist who put forth a mathematical based system of planets going around the sun.

___ 4. Studied the solar system with his telescope and proposed a controversial sun-centered solar system.

___ 5. Astronomer who helped build telescopes and discovered several nebulae, star clusters, and comets.

___ 6. Philosopher who established the scientific method of experimentation and reasoning.

___ 7. Scientist who changed views on time, gravity, and conversion of matter into energy.

___ 8. Physicist who developed quantum theory, changing how atomic and subatomic particles are understood.

___ 9. Established the mathematical foundation for genetics.

___ 10. British scientist who laid the foundation for modern physics.

___ 11. Much of our understanding of electronics is based on this scientist's work with electricity and magnetism.

___ 12. Physicist who discovered radioactive elements and X-rays.

86

Not all learners are strong readers, so a page of print like this might be overwhelming for those who have not had much school success or for those who struggle with tracking across the page. Another option is to do this page together, with you reading the text as learners follow. Or put the names of the scientists on note cards and what they discovered on another note card and have learners physically put them together.

Christianity and Science

Each of the scientific concepts below have been used to support Christianity. Select one of the arguments and explain how it can be used to support the teaching of the faith.

Teleology

Intelligent Design

Second Law of Thermodynamics

Biogenesis

87

Teleology
The intricate design found in all living things points to a Creator.

Intelligent Design
This worldview claims that a creator designed all things. While supporters of this concept do not always credit God with His creation, it can be a starting point to show that someone had to exist in the beginning.

Second Law of Thermodynamics
In a closed system, the total energy available constantly grows smaller. Eventually the universe will reach equilibrium. The earth is moving from a state of order at its beginning to a state of disorder.

Biogenesis
This principle says that living things cannot come from nonliving matter, which speaks directly against evolution.

This section contains some vocabulary that may be unfamiliar and difficult to read for some of your learners. Don't assume that all of your learners can read and comprehend these sections with no assistance. There is likely a wide variety of academic abilities in your group. Divide learners into small groups that each includes learners with a variety of academic and leadership skills. Notice that some learners might show some disruptive behaviors rather than demonstrate their academic difficulties.

Help learners summarize their viewpoint on science and faith. Don't require them to answer these questions in front of other learners.

Encourage learners to record their science and faith questions in this space.

For learners who struggle to get their thoughts down with paper and pencil, allow them to text you their response or use whatever digital device they favor.

CONNECTIONS

SCIENCE QUESTIONS

Many early scientists began their work in an attempt to better understand the created world around them. These men and women saw no conflict between their faith and their studies. Over time, this viewpoint changed, and many modern scientists reject any religious involvement.

So how can you balance your faith with the teachings of science?

My Questions

88

CHECKS FOR UNDERSTANDING

Before your learners leave, consider ways you can give them feedback for next week.

- **Learning Log:** Encourage learners to further research one of the scientists discussed in this lesson and summarize their discoveries in their Learning Log.
- **Exit Ticket:** Have learners write a note with one question they have about science and faith.

Why Do Bad Things Happen?

Timeless Truth

God has called me to be His own and uses me to witness the truth in love with my neighbor.

Lesson Focus

The learner will witness to the fact that although we live in a fallen world because of sin, God will restore all things through the victory He gives in Christ.

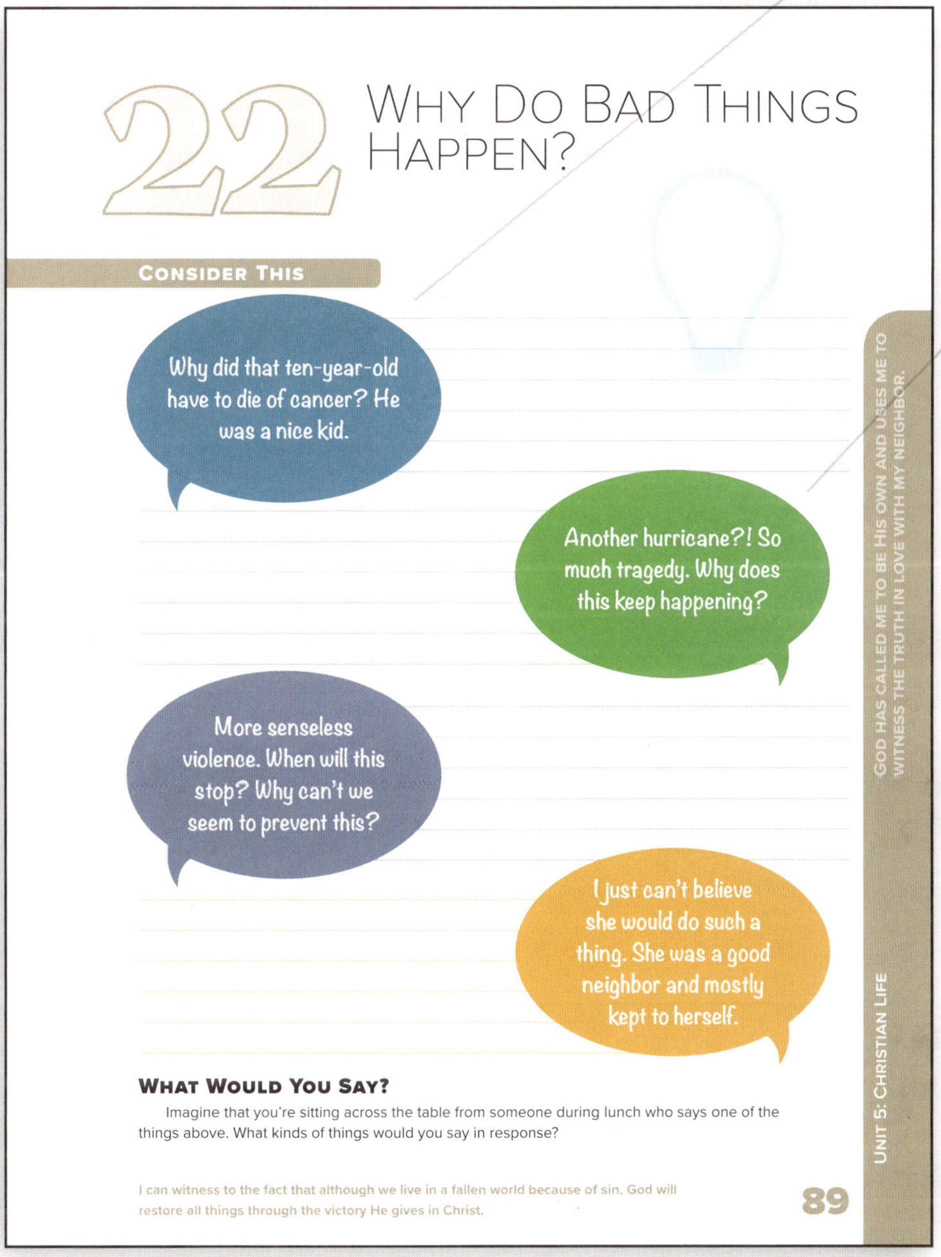

22 Why Do Bad Things Happen?

Consider This

Why did that ten-year-old have to die of cancer? He was a nice kid.

Another hurricane?! So much tragedy. Why does this keep happening?

More senseless violence. When will this stop? Why can't we seem to prevent this?

I just can't believe she would do such a thing. She was a good neighbor and mostly kept to herself.

What Would You Say?

Imagine that you're sitting across the table from someone during lunch who says one of the things above. What kinds of things would you say in response?

I can witness to the fact that although we live in a fallen world because of sin, God will restore all things through the victory He gives in Christ.

89

God has called me to be His own and uses me to witness the truth in love with my neighbor.

Unit 5: Christian Life

You may want to invite learners to create skits in groups, sharing the discussion possibilities with the class during role play.

These examples are just a small sampling of concerns or questions learners may have. If time allows, ask learners to add questions they or others may have about bad things that happen in our world. Invite other learners to add their responses to each of these new statements.

This would be a great time to listen to a dynamic reading of Genesis 3. There are many free options available online, especially as videos.

Obvious answers will include a lack of sin, death, fighting, and the like.

Help learners consider other things that they may fail to notice: Clothes would not wear out. We would not need traffic lights. Homework would always be perfect. Cars would always work properly. Really, we see small tragedies every day, but we take them for granted.

Digging Deeper

Evil Exists

There are some in society today who don't like to use the word *evil*. In fact, they don't believe that evil exists at all. Just a day's worth of news, however, shows proof that evil is a reality. If it wasn't, things would be perfect all the time. Bad things happen, and they continue to happen no matter how hard people try to make things better. (Yes, that sounds like a huge chunk of bad news. Keep going . . .)

Fallen World

It's time once again to go back to the Book of Genesis. When Adam and Eve sinned, creation changed forever. In fact, the mere existence of evil is tragic evidence that something went wrong. If sin hasn't entered the world, why are people so cruel to one another?

Read or listen to **Genesis 3**.

For those who believe that Adam and Eve exist and sinned, the origin of evil makes sense. It's no less terrible, but it's not so surprising. We know bad things do and will happen.

For those who don't believe in those first chapters of Genesis, evil simply doesn't make sense. If everyone is basically good, why don't we just keep acting better? Why would people choose to be bad?

Fallen Creation

When sin entered the world, it messed up everything. Try to imagine for a moment a world without any problems—a world of perfection. What would be different?

90

These pages are not intended for learners to read independently. You can read them aloud or ask volunteers to read aloud.

Groaning Creation

So why do bad things happen? Sometimes, it's merely the result of a world burdened with the weight of sin. When disasters occur, we know it's because we live in a fallen world. It's also a foreshadowing that creation is yearning for the day when Jesus comes back and restores everything to the way it should be.

Read or listen to **Romans 8:18–25**.

Now there's a very big distinction we need to make here. Natural disasters occur because of sin. But they *do not* necessarily occur because of a *particular* sin. In other words, it is dangerous to claim that a certain disaster occurred because of a specific societal sin. Yes, in the Bible, God sometimes tells us of His judgment on sin through disaster. But in those instances, He specifically makes it clear to the people through His Word. So unless God proclaims to us that He's pronouncing a specific judgment, we dare not assume so when bad things happen.

Death and Decay

Because of sin, we die. And not only do people die but plants and animals die too. We all age and decay as death draws near. Our bodies don't work as they should.

Think about all the things that go wrong because of sin. Write down three problems that would not occur if sin was not a part of this world.

Sin's Consequences

There are times when bad things do happen as a result of sin. People filled with evil intent hurt and kill others. People who are reckless sometimes make decisions that harm their life or the lives of others. Yes, there is forgiveness for anyone who sins, but sin still has consequences.

Take, for example, a person who decides to steal a car and then crashes the car into a tree. She could repent and receive forgiveness, but she will still need to serve her time in jail. The car's owner will still need to replace the car. The tree will still die.

When tragedies like this occur, it's tempting for people to put their trust in people. There need to be better rules or education so that this will never happen again, they reason. While we should always strive to improve life for our neighbors, Christians know that no amount of rules will stop the sinful heart from doing wrong.

What other examples of this can you think of?

91

This page reinforces what was discussed on the previous page. If this topic has been thoroughly discussed, you can move forward without much review.

This page throws a great deal of content at the learners and is not intended for them to read independently. Since this page is more informative than interactive, take the time to unpack anything the learners have questions about. If you'd like, invite them to raise their hand as soon as they hear something that confuses them. This can be a quick way to assess prior knowledge and know which learners need extra context.

Connections

Our Enemies

If God is loving, why do bad things happen? The only logical explanation is that God has an enemy.

Satan, the devil, was an angel in heaven named Lucifer. He wanted to take God's place, so he persuaded a third of the angels to try to take over heaven with him, but they lost.

So Satan plotted against God by tempting Adam and Eve. After they ate from the tree of the knowledge of good and evil, they knew sin. They were now sinful, and all humans would now be conceived in sin. Our sinful nature wants to do what is wrong all the time.

Because all people are filled with this sinful nature, the world at large is contrary to God's will. Even when believers are given the gift of the Holy Spirit, they still have to battle against their sinful nature and the sinful nature of everyone else too.

Did you notice the mention of your enemies? Highlight them in the text above: the devil, the world, and our sinful nature.

Our Savior

There's great news, however. Jesus lived as a human, died, and rose again. In so doing, He defeated sin, death, and the devil. The days are numbered for the devil, the world, and our sinful nature. When Jesus comes back, the devil will be completely conquered, the world will be made new, and sinner-saints will be fully saints! (Check out the Apostles' Creed if you want a summary of all this.)

What Now?

It's heartbreaking when bad things happen. There's no getting around that. But we Christians know the beginning of the story of why evil exists. Better yet, we know the end of the story. We know that bad things will continue to happen, but we do not lose hope and we do not give up. What can we Christians do to address the reality of evil in the world?

Make a Plan

Turn back to the first page of this lesson, and choose another speech bubble to address.

92

Checks for Understanding

Before your learners leave, consider ways you can give them feedback for next week.

- **Learning Log:** In their Learning Log, have learners write a response to the question, "Why is there evil?"
- **Video Interview:** As learners leave, take a video of them answering this question: "What can we do when bad things happen?" Send the video out to the learners and their families with a follow-up question: "When we address evil in the world today, how does that witness to God's promise of restoration?"

Are We Alone? What about Demons and Angels?

Timeless Truth

God has called me to be His own and uses me to witness the truth in love with my neighbor.

Lesson Focus

The learner will share that there are nonphysical creatures: angels who serve God and demons who try to lead us away from God.

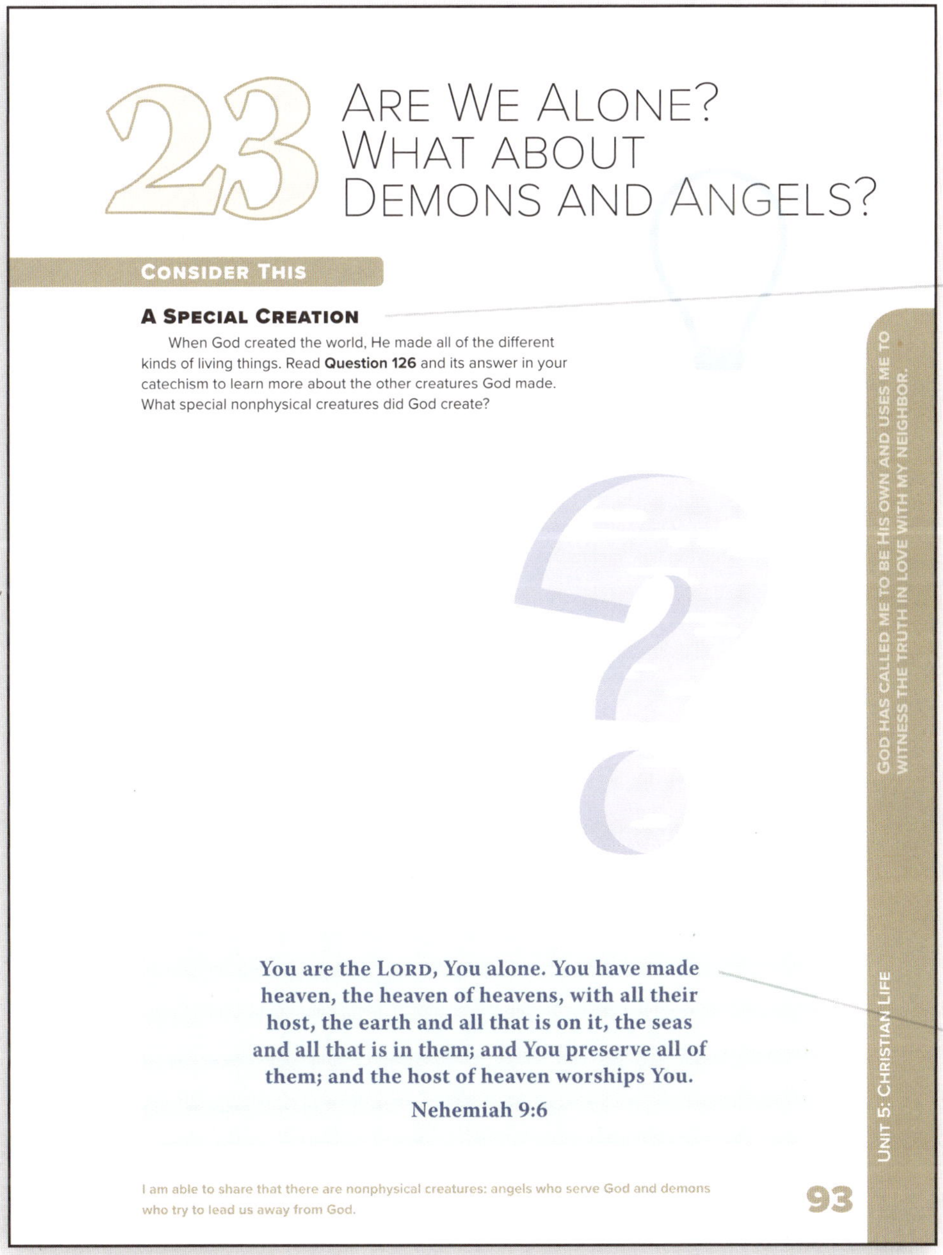

23 Are We Alone? What about Demons and Angels?

Consider This

A Special Creation

When God created the world, He made all of the different kinds of living things. Read **Question 126** and its answer in your catechism to learn more about the other creatures God made. What special nonphysical creatures did God create?

You are the Lord, You alone. You have made heaven, the heaven of heavens, with all their host, the earth and all that is on it, the seas and all that is in them; and You preserve all of them; and the host of heaven worships You.

Nehemiah 9:6

I am able to share that there are nonphysical creatures: angels who serve God and demons who try to lead us away from God.

93

God has called me to be His own and uses me to witness the truth in love with my neighbor.

Unit 5: Christian Life

Option: Ask learners to speculate about why people are so fascinated with angels and demons.

Nehemiah 9:6 points out the angels as God's special nonphysical creation.

The catechism provides information about the origin and purpose of God's angels. They serve God as His messengers and servants, and through them God's people are protected from danger. The angels also continuously worship and praise God.

Allow learners to work in pairs or small groups, making sure that groups have a mixture of learners with a variety of academic and leadership abilities.

Digging Deeper

All about Angels

Question 128 in the Small Catechism explains the origin and work of God's angels. Read through that question and its answer and Bible verses; then, summarize the information in the frame, using words or drawings.

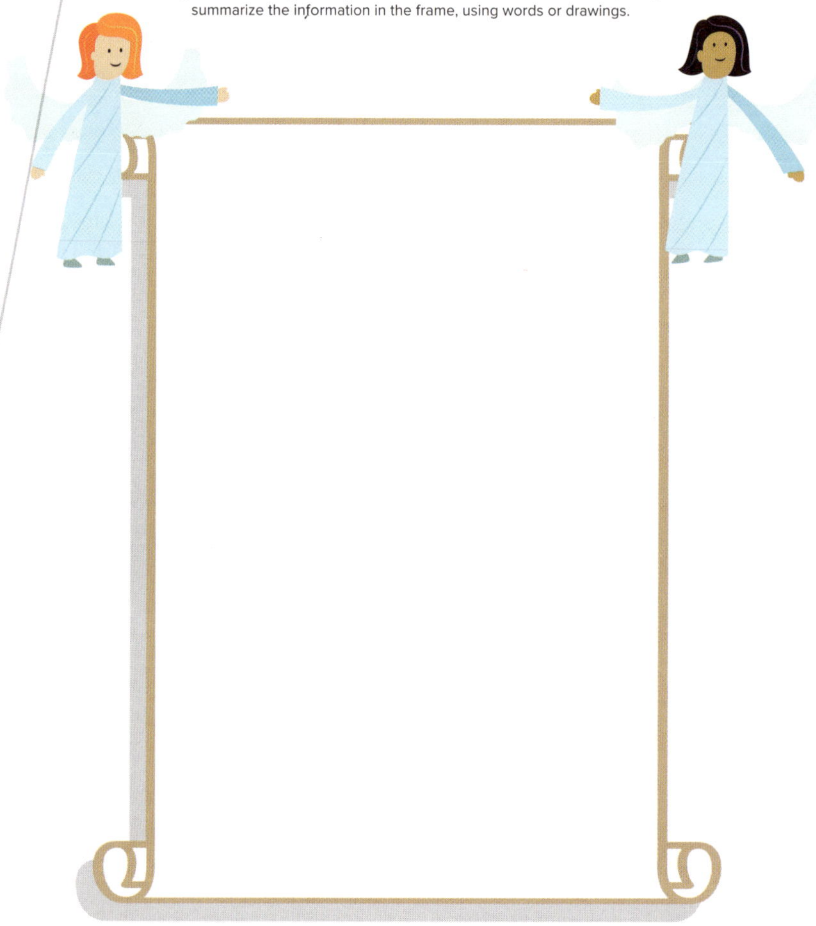

94

DEMONS AND DARKNESS

Are there really demons? If so, where did they come from? Catechism **Question 129** addresses the angels who do not serve God's intended function. Jude 6 clearly tells us how some of the angels rebelled against God, left their proper place, and now reside in darkness as they work against God's plan for His people.

Read or listen to the suggested verses with **Question 129** and then choose one to write in the Bible outline below. Feel free to illustrate your verse or highlight key words.

For we do not wrestle against flesh and blood, but against the rulers, against the authorities, against the cosmic powers over this present darkness, against the spiritual forces of evil in the heavenly places.

Ephesians 6:12

95

Have learners work through Question 129 and select a verse to highlight in their learner book. Summarize the very real nature of demons, who work against God's people. While we need not fear the demons, we need to be aware of their presence and God's promise to protect His people from Satan and his demons.

For learners who aren't strong readers, help them use a Bible app to listen to the verses listed in the catechism; or you can read the verses aloud for the class.

Do we become angels when we die?
The short answer is no. The Bible clearly tells us that we will be raised with new, glorified bodies.

Are we to look to angels for direction in our lives or pray to them?
No. We pray only to God.

Do I have a personal guardian angel?
The Bible doesn't tell us directly, but it does tell us that angels protect God's people.

Learners' personal questions will vary. Be prepared to deal with difficult questions participants may have. It's okay to tell learners that you don't have the answer right now, but then talk to your pastor and return to the questioner with the answer.

CONNECTIONS

WATCHING OVER YOU

Read **Question 130** in the Small Catechism—some of the common questions people ask about angels. Read or listen to the suggested Bible verses and summarize your answers to the questions below.

Do we become angels when we die?

Are we to look to angels for direction in our lives or pray to them?

Do I have a personal guardian angel?

My personal question:

96

Allow learners to work in small groups to answer these questions. Give them time and space to write or tell you their own personal question.

CHECKS FOR UNDERSTANDING

Before your learners leave, consider ways you can give them feedback for next week.

- **Learning Log:** In their Learning Log, have learners record a prayer asking God for strength for those times when they are tempted to follow the leading of Satan and his demons.
- **Exit Ticket:** Have learners record a time when God protected them from danger. Use these as prayer starters during future lessons.

Are We Alone? What about Ghosts and Aliens?

Timeless Truth

God has called me to be His own and uses me to witness the truth in love with my neighbor.

Lesson Focus

The learner will be able to explain that ghosts and aliens are deceptions created to distract from the true God.

24 Are We Alone? What about Ghosts and Aliens?

Consider This

Ghostly Glow

Picture this: you're sitting around the campfire at summer camp. It's dark and quiet, and before too long someone starts telling some creepy ghost stories. You wonder, is there really such a thing as a ghost? What does the Bible have to say about ghosts?

Ghost stories are just that—stories. Scripture tells us that when people die, they go to heaven or hell; they do not linger to communicate with the living or to haunt them. However, the devil is described in 1 Peter 5:8 as our enemy who seeks to devour us. Satan is tricky and wily and would love for people to believe that ghosts are real—because that would mean that heaven and hell are not real.

Read the verse below and share what you think it is telling you about ghosts.

Option: Ask learners to share their favorite "ghost" stories and share what they like about them.

And just as it is appointed for man to die once, and after that comes judgment, so Christ, having been offered once to bear the sins of many, will appear a second time, not to deal with sin but to save those who are eagerly waiting for Him.

Hebrews 9:27–28

God has called me to be His own and uses me to witness the truth in love with my neighbor.

Unit 5: Christian Life

I am able to explain that ghosts and aliens are deceptions created to distract from the true God.

97

1 Corinthians 15:3–6
Christ died and was raised again; those who have died are referred to as having "fallen asleep."

1 Corinthians 15:20–22
Christ is the first to have awakened from the dead; through His death and resurrection, we receive the gift of eternal life with Him.

1 Corinthians 15:42–44
Our natural bodies will be replaced with spiritual bodies.

1 Corinthians 15:50–57
Our earthly bodies are perishable but will be replaced with imperishable bodies at the second coming of Christ.

The Scriptures are very clear that those who die "fall asleep" in Christ. The Bible does not support the concept of ghosts hanging around to wrap up unfinished business. Likewise, the Hollywood invention of zombies and undead are equally fictional and unbiblical.

Digging Deeper

Ghosts, Zombies, and Otherwise Undead

The apostle Paul addresses the issue of death and resurrection in his first letter to the Church at Corinth. Read each of these verses and summarize what it tells about death and life after death. How do these verses speak against the man-made concepts of ghosts, zombies, and otherwise undead?

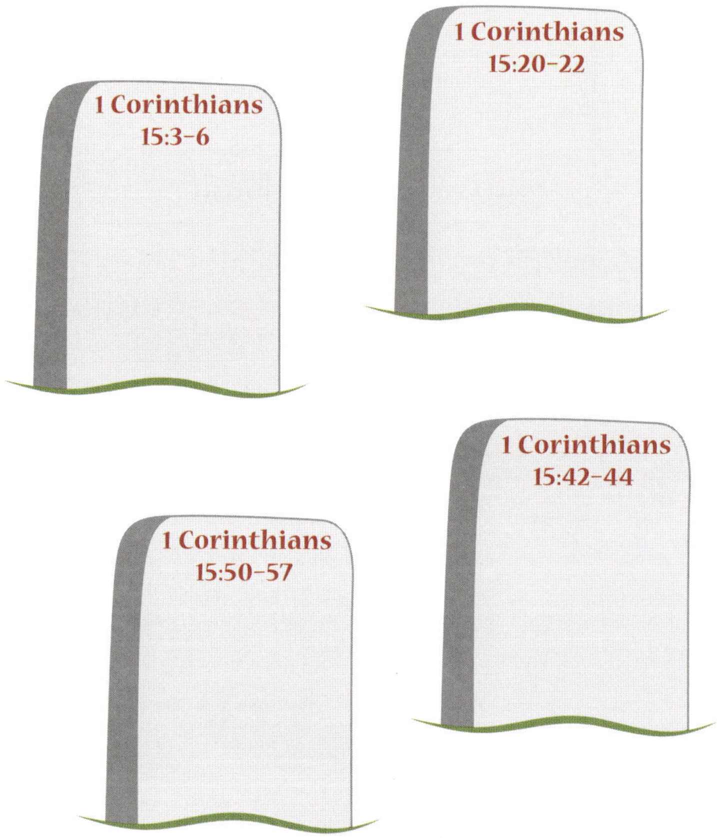

98

To save time, use a sticky note to mark these Scripture passages in a few Bibles. Or allow learners to listen to these passages on a Bible app.

Some learners may struggle to summarize and write in these small spaces. Allow learners to tell you answers or write them on another piece of paper.

ALIEN INVASION

Many people are skeptical about the concept of extraterrestrial life. Yet our world has a fascination with science fiction. Book and movie series like *Star Wars* fuel this fascination. Label each of the alien outlines below with a character, movie title, or book from a science-fiction series.

99

Let learners have fun with this activity. Accept all reasonable responses. However, don't let this activity eat up too much of your lesson time.

As learners are working on these, ask them what intrigues them about these creatures, why people are drawn to the scary creatures, why they enjoy the heroic characters, and how or if they ever feel like it connects to their faith life.

People cannot make themselves perfect. Our only perfection is found in the death and resurrection of Christ. And Scripture is clear that people are created by God.

Scripture clearly tells us that only the Father knows the time of the second coming of Christ. We must keep our focus on Christ rather than the distractions of false teaching.

This kind of search is pointless. Truth is found only in God's Word.

If you have time, have learners practice what they might say to friends and family who genuinely believe in the existence of ghosts and aliens. Role playing is a great way to do this type of practice.

Connections

UFOs and You

There are three basic theories concerning the existence of aliens and UFOs. Read the description of each theory and consider the errors in each.

A New Age?

Some followers of modern, or New Age, religions think they can become perfect on their own or by receiving assistance from science, dead people, and aliens. One modern religion, Scientology, even claims that people were brought to earth in spaceships millions of years ago.

Conspiracy?

The government has scientific advances and secrets concerning alien life forms that they are withholding from the public.

End of the World?

Believers in this theory interpret portions of the Book of Revelation as saying that aliens, or perhaps fallen angels, will return at a time that has been revealed to them.

Make a Plan

This lesson covers a whole lot. You may know people who believe different things about all these topics. Make a plan for how you will answer questions that friends or family may bring up about ghosts, zombies, and aliens.

Start by first writing what you think those questions or beliefs might be. Then, write your planned response.

Think About It . . .

How does spending too much time on these topics distract us from God and His Word? Who is the author of that deception or distraction?

100

Checks for Understanding

Before your learners leave, consider ways you can give them feedback for next week.

- **Learning Log:** In their Learning Log, have learners record one or more Bible verses that remind us of God's promise of eternal life with Him.
- **Quiz Questions:** Have learners write a question for this lesson. Use these questions to review this lesson at the beginning of your next class session.

Is There a Hell? Is There a Heaven?

Timeless Truth

God has called me to be His own and uses me to witness the truth in love with my neighbor.

Lesson Focus

The learner will witness to the facts that hell is a place created for the devil and his demons, and that Jesus rescues us from hell, which we deserve, and welcomes us to be with Him in heaven, which will be made new.

25 Is There a Hell? Is There a Heaven?

Consider This

What If?

What if there were no hell? What if there were no heaven? How would that change the way you lived your life?

Imagine This

You're on a trip, and your GPS system is telling you where to go. Then it speaks this unusual direction: "Cavernous hole in five miles. Detour at the next available right."

That seems odd, you think. You've never heard of a cavernous hole in the middle of the road before. You turn on the radio and get lots of conflicting reports. One news station says that a sinkhole opened up overnight in the region in which you are driving. Another station is doing an opinion piece as to whether the sinkhole should have opened or not. A notification pops up on your phone from an app that says that there is no hole at all, that it is just an attempt at creating a stir and getting attention.

You decide to pass up the detour, despite the GPS chimes and directions. No one seems to be taking it seriously anyway.

An electronic road sign one mile later reads, "GIANT HOLE. TURN AROUND." You roll your eyes and pass the sign.

One mile farther, you come upon a small town. At the stoplight, a group of people run up to you, telling you to avoid the hole that just opened up a few miles away. You thank them and refuse their suggestion to take a break for lunch while everything is sorted out.

Eventually, you see the hole looming in front of you, but you're still pretty sure that the existence of a hole like this defies what you want to think about the world. You keep driving.

I can witness to the facts that hell is a place created for the devil and his demons, and that Jesus rescues us from hell, which we deserve, and welcomes us to be with Him in heaven, which will be made new.

101

God has called me to be His own and uses me to witness the truth in love with my neighbor.

Unit 5: Christian Life

Read this story aloud to your group. Use a bit of a dramatic flair to your voice to make it more interesting. Of if you have a class member who is particularly good at that type of reading, have that learner read it or record it for you prior to class and listen as if it is a radio drama.

These passages are loaded with a great deal of information. You may decide to work through these slowly together. You could also divide them up and ask groups to present assigned readings for the class.

Remind learners who struggle with reading from the Bible to use a Bible app to find and listen to Scripture quickly.

Digging Deeper

Why Does Hell Exist?

Regardless of how we feel about it, hell's existence cannot be ignored. If those around you are wondering about hell, they likely realize the importance of the question. But if people believe in a one-dimensional God who is only love, they'll likely ask why hell exists at all.

Let's take a look at the authority on God's will, the Bible.

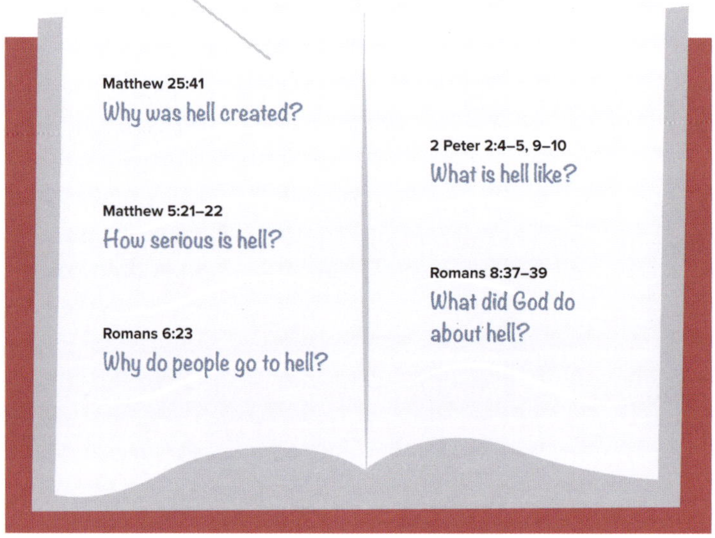

Think About It . . .

How does knowing that hell exists impact the way you think about sharing the Word of God with others?

What Is Heaven Like?

What images or thoughts come to mind when you think of heaven?

Now, Not Yet

Those who have died in the faith are with the Lord. But that's not the end of the story! Someday, all believers will have their bodies and souls reunited. Heaven and earth will be made new. It's wonderful to rest in the Lord now, but it gets even better on the Last Day! Read through these verses, and try to sketch a picture of what you think the new creation may look like.

Isaiah 25:8–9
John 14:1–6
1 Thessalonians 4:13–18
Revelation 21:1–7
Revelation 22:1–6

103

Essentially, this page is a pre- and post-assessment tool. In other words, after your learners have drawn both images, compare how the second image changed after reading the Bible passages.

Remember to use a Bible app to help learners locate and listen to Scripture passages quickly and easily, especially those who struggle with reading.

"The next time it comes up?" your learners might ask. "But we just talked about the importance of telling people about hell!"

This sort of question can be a great discussion starter about the tension between the urgency of the Gospel and the approach we take with those who might be resistant to the Gospel. The approach will depend on the person in mind.

CONNECTIONS

WARNING SIGNS

Sometimes, people don't want to think about hell because they don't want to worry about who might be there. It's one of the hardest truths we have to face: Some people choose to not listen to the Word of God, and God will not force anyone to live with Him for eternity. There is a terrible punishment for sin, and we all deserve it. But God's love is boundless.

> *This is good, and it is pleasing in the sight of God our Savior, who desires all people to be saved and to come to the knowledge of the truth. For there is one God, and there is one mediator between God and men, the man Christ Jesus, who gave Himself as a ransom for all, which is the testimony given at the proper time.*
>
> 1 Timothy 2:3–5

Hell and sin and death are uncomfortable topics, but ignoring them doesn't make them go away. Instead, out of love for others, God sends us out to tell of Jesus, the Savior of all. Like the driver who ignores the GPS warnings, not everyone will listen as we talk about Jesus and His plan of salvation. But we can listen to God's Word and share it with everyone we can.

SUM IT UP

Think of someone you know who doesn't believe in heaven or hell. What are things you can practice saying for the next time it comes up?

104

CHECKS FOR UNDERSTANDING

Before your learners leave, consider ways you can give them feedback for next week.

- **Learning Log:** Have learners record verses from the Book of Revelation that describe heaven in their Learning Log.
- **Exit Ticket:** Ask learners to illustrate their concept of what heaven looks like.

What about Miracles?

Timeless Truth

God has called me to be His own and uses me to witness the truth in love with my neighbor.

Lesson Focus

The learner will share examples of how God uses ordinary means to aid us in times of need now and in the future.

26 WHAT ABOUT MIRACLES?

CONSIDER THIS

It's a Miracle!

Throughout the Bible, we read accounts of victory in battle, physical healing, and God's control over the very forces of nature. In the space below, list some of the miracles you recall from Scripture. According to **Hebrews 2:3–4**, what is one of the purposes of these miracles?

It was declared at first by the Lord, and it was attested to us by those who heard, while God also bore witness by signs and wonders and various miracles and by gifts of the Holy Spirit distributed according to His will.

Hebrews 2:3–4

GOD HAS CALLED ME TO BE HIS OWN AND USES ME TO WITNESS THE TRUTH IN LOVE WITH MY NEIGHBOR.

UNIT 5: CHRISTIAN LIFE

I can share examples of how God uses ordinary means to aid us in times of need now and in the future.

105

Spend a brief time reviewing the list of miracles learners come up with.

The words of Hebrews remind us that God uses miracles to reveal Jesus to us as well as to benefit His people.

If writing is an impediment to participation for some learners, use this activity as a discussion starter rather than a writing task.

Faith does not demand a miracle, nor does faith compel God to perform a miracle.

Matthew 9:27–30
When the blind men affirm their trust, Jesus tells them it will be done as their faith desires.

Mark 5:25–34
Jesus tells the woman her faith has made her well.

Matthew 15:28
Jesus tells a Canaanite woman that her faith is great as He heals her daughter.

Mark 9:20–27
A man seeking to have Jesus heal his son tells Jesus, "I believe; help my unbelief."

Help learners understand that there is a connection between faith and miracles. Also remind them that faith is not a work that we do but a gift of God.

Again, if reading and writing are an impediment to participation and learning for students, turn this into a verbal group activity, with you or another strong reader reading the Scripture passages.

Digging Deeper

Miracles and Faith

The relationship between miracles and faith is rooted in the Scriptures. Read each of the miracle accounts below and jot down a brief summary of the connection between the miracle and faith.

Matthew 9:27–30

Mark 5:25–34

Matthew 15:28

Mark 9:20–27

106

Modern-Day Miracles

Some people question whether miracles still occur today. These individuals claim that since the close of the New Testament era, the time of miracles has ended.

Today God chooses to work through means, through the physical elements of our world and through the many and various vocations God gives people. Take a look at each of the areas where God acts through means to work what might seem ordinary, but that in reality are actually quite miraculous.

Consider how God uses vocations and everyday elements in each of the areas below and jot down a few notes about or discuss these modern-day miracles.

Medical Miracles

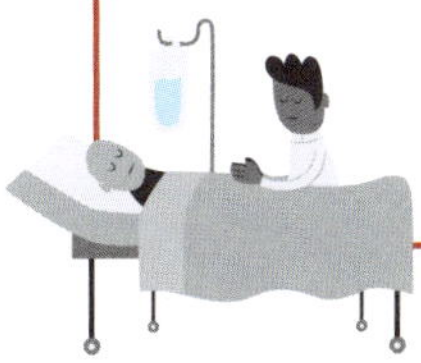

Food Miracles

Everyday Miracles

107

Medical Miracles

God uses doctors, nurses, and scientists to help us heal and to find cures for many different diseases.

Food Miracles

Farmers, bakers, truckers, grocery store workers, and others all ease the process of getting food to our table at home.

Everyday Miracles

Answers will vary in this section. It could include modern transportation, computers, phones, hearing aids, antibiotics, insect control, or any number of things.

Not getting the answer to prayer that we desire can be extremely difficult, especially when our prayer involves someone we love and care for. But sometimes God has a different plan. As Christians, we know that God cares about our eternal life. So when a Christian friend dies, we know that God has a better plan for that person. God chose to take that person home to be with Himself.

We can never fully understand God's plan for us, but we can be assured that He gives us full and free salvation and life eternal through the death and resurrection of His own Son.

CONNECTIONS

WHEN MIRACLES DON'T HAPPEN

So what about when a miracle doesn't happen? Does this mean that God can't or doesn't want to heal your friend with cancer? Or what about the time you really prayed for something but you didn't get it?

To ask the catechism question, "What does this mean?" How do we deal with miracles that don't happen?

In Luther's explanation to the Introduction to the Lord's Prayer, he talks about God's love for His children and His work in our lives. Ultimately, God will provide healing for our sinful, broken bodies and for our souls in heaven. How can this reassure believers?

God has created, redeemed, and called me to be His own.

God has a plan for me as His human creature.

108

CHECKS FOR UNDERSTANDING

Before your learners leave, consider ways you can give them feedback for next week.

- **Learning Log:** In their Learning Log, have learners write the names of people they know who use their vocations to bring health and healing today.
- **Reflect and Review:** Have learners write down the people God uses to carry out modern-day miracles and then share their ideas with a classmate.

What Does God Want Me to Do as a Christian?

Timeless Truth

God has called me to be His own and uses me to witness the truth in love with my neighbor.

Lesson Focus

The learner will be able to tell that he or she is redeemed and free to love God and others, and equipped by God to serve his or her neighbor and tell others about Jesus.

This lesson is deeply connected to Lesson 19, regarding identity. In case it isn't obvious to learners, reinforce that we can only talk about loving our neighbor because we are redeemed and have the Holy Spirit living in us. If they don't understand that, they will view this lesson as hopelessly focused on our works. Carefully listen to your learners' comments today, guiding them toward this understanding.

27 What Does God Want Me to Do as a Christian?

Consider This

You just had the most amazing dinner in your life. Every bite was incredible, the service was perfect, and the ambiance was just right. Even better, the dinner was free! Someone else paid the bill and will pay the bill for everyone else too. What do you do?

You've read the best book ever. It literally has changed your life. You'll never look at the world the same again. And this book is all over the place; you have plenty of copies. What do you do?

You were trapped. You were with a group on a hike, and the ground fell out from underneath you. Debris covered up the opening, and you couldn't see anything. You and everyone else with you were deep in a cavernous hole, with no hope of rescue. Suddenly, a rock moved away from above you, and you were all quickly pulled out of certain death. What do you do?

You were a criminal. You know that what you did deserved the death sentence, and there's no way around it. You're in a room full of cells holding prisoners who are expecting the same fate. In the middle of the night, the executioner walks into the room and unlocks every door. Noticing that you are awake, he mutters, "You've been set free, all of you." Then, he leaves without another word. What do you do?

Instead of reading these scenarios independently, have learners work together in pairs or small groups to read them together and then share with the entire group. Be sensitive to learners who struggle with reading and are uncomfortable sharing that information with peers.

Think About It . . .

All of these stories are amazing, but none of them comes close to the unfathomable grace God gives to each one of us. So what do you do?

GOD HAS CALLED ME TO BE HIS OWN AND USES ME TO WITNESS THE TRUTH IN LOVE WITH MY NEIGHBOR.

UNIT 5: CHRISTIAN LIFE

I am able to tell that I am redeemed and free to love God and others, and equipped by God to serve my neighbor and tell others about Jesus.

109

Point to the illustration of the Christian. In God's eyes, we are forgiven and holy. There is nothing we can do, aside from unbelief, to take away God's love or forgiveness. Free in that grace, we go out to others and love them by witness and service.

This page is not intended to be read independently by the learner. Use the text as a guideline and for the basis of discussion.

Use a bookmark or sticky note to mark the end of each Gospel in your Bible or in several Bibles for your class.

Apologetics serves as a tool of evangelism, but never as the first approach. One should only apply apologetics when issues are raised. Always lead with the Law and the Gospel.

Digging Deeper

Saved! Now What?

You've just received the most incredible gift ever! You fully deserved to die and suffer an eternity of punishment. Instead, God Himself died in your place and rose again, conquering the sin and death that had threatened to claim you. He loves you dearly and has claimed you as His precious child. Now, you will live forever in the most beautiful place imaginable. Better yet, He loves and has died for everyone. So what do you do?

Go . . .

After Jesus rose from the dead, but before He ascended into heaven, He gave instructions to His followers: Go and tell. Go and teach. I am sending you.

Turn to the last several verses of each Gospel to see what Jesus had to say. (If your Bible has red letters for Jesus, it will be pretty simple!)

So if we're to go and tell, how do we do that? What have we learned about defending the faith? Why is it so important for us to share the Gospel?

110

Love

As forgiven children of God, it is our joy to obey the Lord. He has given us His Commandments, which are good as guides for daily life, as witnesses to God's will, and as helps as we serve our neighbor. Jesus summarized the Ten Commandments by telling us to love God and love our neighbor (see **Matthew 22:37–39**). So really, the greatest command is to love (check out **1 Corinthians 13:13**).

How do we show our love? What are different ways we can show our love? Check out the Table of Duties in the Small Catechism. Also use the Ten Commandments as your guide. Write down some ways that you, specifically, can show love to others.

What are three things people learn when they live their life for others?

111

It may be strange, but the Law is summed up in one word: *love* (see the passages on the next page, for example). Love is also the heart of the Gospel, because God first loved us.

Your learners may be at different levels of ability to work independently on these types of questions. Give guidance and coach individuals through these sections as needed.

There is not a magical list of three, so invite brainstorm options. Be sure that they include a witness to Jesus as Savior. Also, we witness to God's will for our lives. When we love others and work for healing and restoration, we are pointing to our hope in the eternal restoration on the Last Day. Serving selflessly is countercultural and will often catch attention.

For learners who struggle with Bible reading, prepare these Scripture verses on note cards prior to class. Help learners use a Bible app to listen to Scripture when reading skills are weak.

Early on in this course, there was an invitation to create a nickname or team name for your class. Perhaps you've been keeping that up throughout the course. If so, consider making a poster with a team mission statement. If your church or school has a theme or statement, discuss that as well.

CONNECTIONS

KNOW YOUR WHY

What do these Bible verses have to say about God's love for us and for all people?

1 John 4:19

Ephesians 2:8–10

John 13:34–35

John 20:19–21

Groups, teams, and businesses often have a mission statement, something that helps define who they are and why they do what they do. Answer these questions and come up with your own personal mission statement.

- Who are you?
- What do you do?
- Why do you do what you do?

Use those answers to write a mission statement:

AS A ______________________________,
I WILL ______________________________
BECAUSE I ______________________________
____
______________________________.

In a way, the best way to defend the faith is to live it out in the places God puts us. How do we do that? Think about things you can do in your callings, your vocations, to witness to others.

112

CHECKS FOR UNDERSTANDING

Before your learners leave, consider ways you can give them feedback for next week.

- **Personal Mission:** If time runs short, or perhaps to extend the lesson, invite learners to work on their mission statements at home. They could create a poster or a T-shirt (using permanent or fabric markers) and bring them in next week.
- **Learning Log:** Ask the essential question for this unit: What is God's will for me as I live the Christian life?

What Does God Say about Marriage?

Timeless Truth

God has called me to be His own and uses me to witness the truth in love with my neighbor.

Lesson Focus

The learner will describe that God is the creator and authority for marriage, which is a picture of Christ and His Church.

28 What Does God Say about Marriage?

Consider This

In a Perfect World . . .

If you could have a perfect world, what would it be like?

In God's Perfect World . . .

If we want to see what God considers a perfect world, we need look no further than Genesis 1–2, where we read about the perfect world He created. What do we know about life in the Garden of Eden? Read or listen to **Genesis 1–2** if you need reminders.

God created the perfect marriage too. What did it look like?

God has called me to be His own and uses me to witness the truth in love with my neighbor.

Unit 5: Christian Life

I can describe that God is the creator and authority for marriage, which is a picture of Christ and His Church.

113

Today, keep in mind that many of your learners will have firsthand experience with cohabitation and divorce. It's also very likely that they know someone who embraces a homosexual lifestyle. God's truth told in love is a key theme today for the learners!

Allow and encourage learners to draw their responses when writing gets in the way of thinking.

You may want to decide ahead of time which catechism questions your learners need to review especially. Or simply read each question (without reading the answers) and ask learners to write down the numbers of the questions they want to discuss.

If your learners already went through a catechism study, this can be a review. If not, this may take the majority of the lesson today.

Digging Deeper

Fallen Creation

Ever since the fall, humans have decided that they know better than God when it comes to . . . well, everything. What are some things that humans say about a perfect world that differ from God's creation?

Marriage Is a Gift from God

God made marriage. As much as we'd like to tell Him what marriage should look like, He's the one who made it, so He gets to decide what it is. It's a beautiful gift! He made man and woman. He made sex. He made a way for children to be born. So, of course, the devil will want to distort this beautiful God-given gift called marriage. Let's refocus and turn off the world's noise for a moment. Let's turn to the Small Catechism and remember what God designed for marriage.

Turn to *Luther's Small Catechism with Explanation*. Look through **Questions 65–77**. As a group, make a list of which of these questions you want to focus on today. Work through these questions together, using the Bible passages given in the catechism.

114

Using Your Tools

Using God's Word, the Small Catechism, and fellow believers, provide responses to the following comments. You may need another sheet of paper for extra writing space today.

Living together before marriage is totally fine, as long as the couple is heterosexual.

If someone is attracted to a person of the same sex, it must be because that's how God made them.

I don't want to get a divorce, so I'm just going to live with my boyfriend. It's less stressful that way.

Pornography doesn't hurt anyone. It's not like I'm actually having sex.

115

Be sure to point out that Christians who condone some sexual sins but not others are being hypocritical. Also acknowledge that some Christians are tempted to condone all sexual sins to pardon their own. Show how we all need to confess our sins and repent of them before God.

Be sensitive, speaking the truth in love, to learners who have family and close friends who may say exactly what is said in these bubbles.

Also be aware that some learners may have been victimized and are dealing with guilt, shame, and brokenness from the experience, and are in need of the healing and hope offered by the Gospel.

This first comment is a popular one. Show the danger of this rhetoric. Does it apply to many people? to young children? to relatives? to animals? Show how any rhetoric we might want to use for one issue can easily be applied to another. We can't draw the line where we want.

The second comment points to those who truly are cruel to others and separates them from those who, in love, confess God's will for our lives. Christians can be both loving and honest. Review how to speak the truth in love, from Lesson 4, as needed.

This last section gets to the heart of the matter as to why marriage is under such attack and also why Christians consider this to be important. It would be far easier for Christians to ignore these issues and appear to be loving (i.e., accepting). But in love, Christians witness to God's will for marriage as well as to Christ's relationship to us.

CONNECTIONS

Love is the only thing that matters. You should be able to marry anyone you want.

God hates sexual sin! God hates those who sin sexually.

Marriage as a Picture of Christ and His Church

You might be wondering why marriage is such a big deal to God. There are many reasons, but God specifically uses marriage as a constant reminder to His people of the relationship Christ has with His Church. So of course, the devil wants to warp the picture of marriage as much as possible. If Jesus is the Bridegroom and the Church is the Bride, what do the following examples imply about Jesus and His Church?

- A man and a woman don't marry, and they sometimes have relationships with other people.
- A man has many wives.
- A woman has many husbands.
- A man and a woman divorce.
- Two men marry.
- Two women marry.

When marriage is upheld according to God's design, it proclaims that Christ faithfully serves the Church, even to the point of laying down His life for her. It proclaims that the Church loves and obeys Christ, forsaking other gods in faithfulness. Those who serve this way in marriage witness to Christ!

116

Checks for Understanding

Before your learners leave, consider ways you can give them feedback for next week.

- **Class Update:** How did the lesson go today? You may want to summarize the learning and discussion from today by emailing the learners and families for reflection throughout the week. Be prepared that parents may come to you with additional questions or comments.
- **Exit Ticket:** Ask learners to write down a question they still have. If they'd like, they can place their questions in a box. Work through these questions this week and prepare a response to share during the next class.

What Does God Say about Gender Identity?

Timeless Truth

God has called me to be His own and uses me to witness the truth in love with my neighbor.

Lesson Focus

The learner will share with others that God has created him or her uniquely male or female.

This lesson deals with issues related to gender and gender identity. Your learners may be aware of these issues, but the information they have likely comes from worldly sources.

Note: We will not be discussing issues of sexuality or sexual orientation.

29 What Does God Say about Gender Identity?

Consider This

Get Your Xs and Ys in Order!

Are you ready for some science? Every cell in your body contains 46 chromosomes in 23 pairs. One of these pairs determines your sex. Individuals with two X chromosomes are female, while those with one X and one Y are male.

How does science support what the Bible tells us about being male or female?

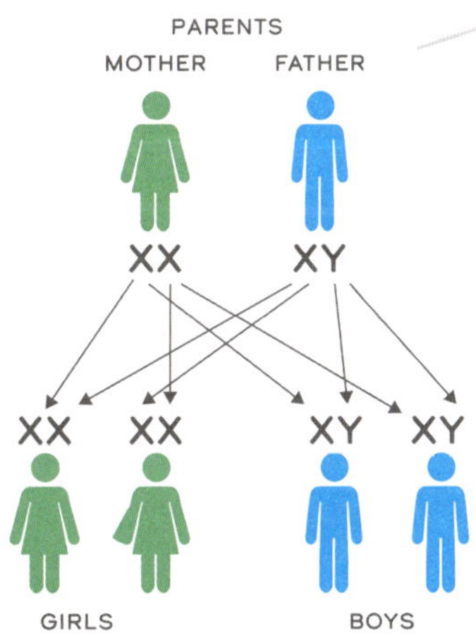

**So God created man in His own image,
in the image of God He created him;
male and female He created them. Genesis 1:27**

**He [Jesus] answered, "Have you not read that
He who created them from the beginning
made them male and female"?
Matthew 19:4**

God has called me to be His own and uses me to witness the truth in love with my neighbor.

Unit 5: Christian Life

I can share with others that God has created me uniquely male/female.

117

Learners may have some background in the science of gender. The diagram helps explain how X and Y chromosomes influence the gender of offspring.

Science confirms exactly what the Bible says about the fact that God created two genders: male and female.

Be prepared for learners who may be aware of rare genetic conditions when the gender of a baby is not easily determined. Be open and honest with learners; these genetic conditions are real, but are also extremely rare (fewer than 1 birth in 100,000).

1. Children who don't fit in often serve as the target for bullies. Sadly, this usually has little to do with their actual gender.

2. Videos of parents celebrating the gender of their yet-to-be-born child abound online. Interestingly, these parents see no difference between sex and gender.

3. Playing sports or being more interested in typically male activities is a stage many young women experience at some point in life. Just because our culture has labeled an activity "male" or "female" does not mean that the person doing them is any more or less male or female. These cultural norms often shift over the course of time.

Digging Deeper

Sex or Gender?

This world is a confusing place. Until recently, when you said someone was male or female, you were talking about that person's biological sex *and* gender. But nowadays, many people in this world confuse or try to separate these two concepts. They would define your biological gender as your "sex" but say that your "gender" is how you choose to express your "maleness" or "femaleness."

How does the confusion in the meaning of these words work with each of these situations?

1. A boy gets bullied by another student for acting "sissy"

2. Expecting parents host a gender-reveal party

3. A girl's parents worry because she only wants to play sports and people typically call her a "tomboy"

118

Living in a Broken World

Face it, we live in a broken, sinful world. It's a world where some people deny their God-given gender and confuse their biological gender with the way they express that gender.

How can you respond to someone who claims that there are more than two genders?

How can you respond to someone who claims to not be the gender he or she was born as?

What are some of the questions you have about the differences between sex and gender?

119

The questions in this section have no easy answers. Be open and caring in your approach to learner concerns.

The concept of more than two genders is in reality a confusion between gender and sexuality.

Dealing with friends who are confused about their gender requires careful conversations to help them understand that you want to keep the conversation open but you don't necessarily agree with their reasoning. Seek help from a trusted adult.

Be prepared to seek additional help from your pastor or other professionals as needed.

As Christians, we find our identity in our Baptism. We bear the very image of God rather than our self-made or societally influenced image.

Allow time for learners to write or draw how they could live out God's plan for their gender.

Be sensitive to comments from uncomfortable kids who try to make jokes or call certain things "boy" jobs or "girl" jobs. Try to turn those conversations toward vocation and how we use our gifts to serve our neighbor.

CONNECTIONS

BEING WHO GOD MADE YOU TO BE

On the first page of this lesson, there are two verses that explain God's plan for His created people. He made you, His child, to be the sex or gender He wanted you to be. How can you live out His plan for you? Use words or drawings to illustrate your thoughts.

120

CHECKS FOR UNDERSTANDING

Before your learners leave, consider ways you can give them feedback for next week.

- **Learning Log:** In the Learning Log, have learners record what makes them a unique creation of God.
- **Prayer Starters:** Have learners write a prayer of thanks to God for the gift of making them uniquely male or female and asking Him to help them live out His plan for their lives.

THINGS TO KNOW WHEN DEFENDING THE FAITH

TIMELESS TRUTH

God has called me to be His own and uses me to witness the truth in love with my neighbor.

LESSON FOCUS

The learner will express that God is with us and gives us what we need to defend the faith and witness to those who need to hear of their Savior.

Hooray! This day can be a celebration, as you've worked together over many tough subjects. Feel free to add to the joyful nature of the lesson, but remind learners that—just like confirmation—this is not a graduation. If anything, it is more like the end of basic training. There is much more ahead! Learners will continue to need the church, teachers, and one another as they live in Christ and share the Gospel with others. If this is this the last class before confirmation, the last lesson of the catechism study course has some sending language that also asserts that this is merely the beginning of learning.

30 THINGS TO KNOW WHEN DEFENDING THE FAITH

CONSIDER THIS

SUM IT UP

Wow! You've made it through this apologetics course. You've tackled some really tough issues, you've considered how to approach God's truth with love, and you've learned a lot. Take a minute to reflect. What important things did you learn? Skim the table of contents if you need help, but don't just copy down the titles of the lessons; share a list of what interesting or helpful things you know now that you didn't know before.

Instead of writing a list, learners can tell you their list while you write it. Or allow learners to use their preferred digital device for typing their response.

GOD HAS CALLED ME TO BE HIS OWN AND USES ME TO WITNESS THE TRUTH IN LOVE WITH MY NEIGHBOR.

UNIT 5: CHRISTIAN LIFE

I can express that God is with me and gives me what I need to defend the faith and witness to those who need to hear of their Savior.

121

Defending the faith can be intimidating! Even though you've worked through thirty lessons together, there will certainly still be a sense of trepidation among your apologists. Let this class ring with the comfort of the Gospel and a knowledge that their callings are from the Lord, who will equip them for the tasks He gives them.

These sections are not meant to be done independently, but with you as leader or by pairs and small groups.

You could also divide your class into groups and have each group take a numbered item.

If learners are struggling with finding verses for the "You Will Not be Perfect" activity, suggest one of these:

- **1 John 1:8–9**
- **Hebrews 4:15**
- **2 Corinthians 5:21**

Digging Deeper

Five Things You Need to Know

In Lesson 27, we reviewed how Jesus wants us to go out and live our lives in Him so that others will learn about Him too. Over the past twenty-nine lessons, you've learned a wealth of information that will hopefully help you as you speak the truth in love to those around you. But as you go out, there are some things to keep in mind.

1 You will not be perfect, and you are forgiven.

You know it, but it's good to remember. You are a sinful human being. You are going to fail. If you try to put pressure on yourself to witness perfectly, you will most definitely be disappointed. But you are also forgiven! Trust that God will use you as He sees fit, and rest in His grace when you mess up. God is bigger than your mistakes.

Are there any Bible verses that would help you keep this in mind?

2 God is with you.

Remember when Jesus told His followers to go out and tell others about Him? He also gave a promise. He said that He would be with them to the end of the age. He also said that He would be sending a Helper, the Holy Spirit. God gives you the words to say in His Bible, and He also guides you as you live in this world.

3 People didn't always listen to Jesus.

Look at the following examples. Jesus applied Law and Gospel perfectly. He spoke and demonstrated the truth in love. He used the Bible. He's God Himself! But still, not everyone listened to Him. God does not force people to listen to Him. We can't either, even if we want to, out of care for them. When people turn away, take heart in the Lord.

122

Read or listen to some of these examples. Why don't people listen?

Mark 10:17–22

John 6:41–64

John 15:18–21

4 You have the tools.

God is with you, and He has given you His Word. That's no small thing! God's Word is perfect and powerful. Also, God's Word does not return empty. Sometimes, that means we need to be patient. Maybe your witness helped someone and you'll never know it. Maybe another Christian will be a witness to that same person later. But regardless, you have what you need to share the Word. Remember Lesson 5? There are other tools God gives too: you have pastors and teachers and other believers. You have the Small Catechism, which helps explain the Word in simple terms. You have a mind and reasoning and other learning that, when used with God's Word, can testify to the truth.

123

Mark 10:17–22
The rich young man feels he has followed all the rules, but his wealth hinders him from following Jesus.

John 6:41–64
Jesus' followers fail to understand His teaching. They are looking for an earthly king who can provide them with food, rather than a heavenly king who will feed their souls.

John 15:18–21
People will not follow Jesus' words because they don't recognize His authority, which comes from the Father.

Save some time at the end of class for learners to decorate this certificate, perhaps while enjoying a snack. Also, this informal time might be an opportunity for learners to talk with you about specific questions and concerns.

CONNECTIONS

5 **DEFEND THE FAITH TO GIVE HOPE.**

Remember the purpose behind the effort. You're not defending the faith to prove yourself right or to shame others. When people learn of and believe in Jesus, they receive the sure hope of eternal life.

Who might need to hear God's Word from you?

For I am not ashamed of the gospel, for it is the power of God for salvation to everyone who believes, to the Jew first and also to the Greek.

Romans 1:16

____

(Name)

DEFENDER OF THE FAITH

124

CHECKS FOR UNDERSTANDING

Before your learners leave, consider ways you can assess learning.

- **Learning Log:** Have learners answer the question, "What is one important thing you learned during this course?"
- **Exit Ticket:** Ask learners to all write their answer to this question on one piece of poster board: "What does it mean to defend the faith?"